Quantitative Analysis with JASP open-source software: Foundational Methods

Christopher P. Halter

Quantitative Analysis

Copyright © 2024 by Christopher P. Halter
All rights reserved. No part of this document may be reproduced or transmitted in any form or by any means, electronic, mechanical, photocopying, recording, or otherwise, without prior written permission of the author

ISBN: 9798327386587

You will be able to explain this so that even your dog understands it.

CONTENTS

SECTION I: OVERVIEW — 1

Chapter 1 The Guide — 2
Notes about the statistics guide — 2

Chapter 2 The Language of Statistical Research — 4
Why use statistics in Social Science research? — 4
What is Continuous and Categorical Data? — 5
Parametric versus Non-Parametric Data — 7
Statistical Assumptions — 8

Chapter 3 Frequentist Statistical Analysis — 11
P-Value — 11
Confidence Intervals (CI) — 12
Effect Size — 15

Chapter 4 Getting Started with JASP — 18
Preparing the Data and Making Decisions — 18
Thinking about Data — 18
Data in JASP — 19
Using .SAV in JASP — 20
Spreadsheets in JASP (.osd & .csv) — 21
Creating .jasp File — 25
Tutorials and Help — 26

SECTION II: DESCRIPTIVE STATISTICS AND DATA VISUALIZATION — 29

Chapter 5 Descriptive Statistics — 30
What are descriptive statistics? — 30
Creating Descriptive Statistics in JASP for Categorical Data — 30
Descriptive Statistics for Continuous Data — 36
Basic Descriptive Statistics — 37
Graphs and Visualizing Continuous Data — 39
Continuous Data SPLIT by Categorical Data — 41

SECTION III: FREQUENTIST APPROACHES — 45

Chapter 6 Relationship Analysis with t-Test — 46
When to use t-Tests – in plain English — 46
t-Test Analysis (Continuous Differences, two groups) — 47
Independent Samples t-Test — 48
Interpreting the Results Tables for Independent Samples t-Test (Directed Reading) — 51
Interpreting the Results Tables for Independent Samples t-Test: Nonparametric Example (Eye Movement) — 53
Paired Samples t-Test — 56

Interpreting the Results Tables for Paired Samples t-Test (Moon & Aggression)	59
One Sample t-Test	61
Interpreting the Results Tables for One Sample t-Test (Directed Reading)	63

Chapter 7 Relationship Analysis with ANOVA — 66

When to use ANOVA – in plain English	66
Analysis of Variance (ANOVA)	66
Using Univariate Analysis for One-Way ANOVA (Parametric Example)	67
Interpreting Results Tables: One-Way ANOVA (Pain Threshold)	71
Using Univariate Analysis for One-Way ANOVA (Non-Parametric Example Kruskal-Wallis)	73
Interpreting Results Tables: One-Way ANOVA (Facebook Friends)	77

Chapter 8 Associations with Correlation — 80

When to use Correlations – in plain English	80
Correlations	81
Correlation Analysis Parametric Data (Parametric Example)	82
Interpreting Results Tables: Correlation Matrix (Auction)	84
Correlation Analysis Nonparametric Data (Nonparametric Example)	85
Interpreting Results Tables: Correlation (Exam Anxiety)	87
Correlation Analysis with Rank Order Data (Nonparametric Example)	89
Interpreting Results Tables: Correlation Matrix (Fear of Statistics)	90

Chapter 9 Associations with Regression (Simple Linear) — 93

When to use Simple Linear Regression – in plain English	93
Regression	93
Simple Linear Regression Analysis	95
Interpreting Results Tables: Simple Linear Regression (Auction)	97

Chapter 10 Relationship Analysis with Contingency Tables — 100

When to Use Contingency Tables – in plain English	100
What is a Contingency Table?	100
Chi-Square Analysis – Test of Independence	101
Using the Contingency Tables in JASP	102
Interpreting Results Tables: Contingency Table Analysis (Health Habits)	104

SECTION IV: RESOURCES — 109

Analysis Memos	110
Data Sets used in the Guide	112
Effect Size Tables	119
Reporting Frequentist Statistics	120
Interpreting Effect Size	123
References	124

THANK YOU.

To the JASP Team at the University of Amsterdam for creating this beautiful, user-friendly application that brings the analysis process to everyone. And to the readers who are on this mathematical journey with us.

Section I: Overview

Chapter 1
The Guide

Notes about the statistics guide

So let's get this out of the way right from the start. This is NOT a math book. I know that you have heard this before but believe me when I say that in this guide you will not have to memorize any formulas.

The JASP Guide's purpose is to assist the novice social science and education researcher in interpreting statistical output data using the JASP Statistical Analysis application. Or, I could say that this guide helps you understand quantitative analysis without the tears. Through the examples and guidance, you will be able to select the statistical test that is appropriate for your data, apply the inferential test to your data, and interpret a statistical test's results table.

In this guide I try to take the novice researcher through the analysis process without relying on the complex mathematical formulas. I use simple to understand, straight forward language to give you a firm foundation in quantitative analysis methods.

The Guide goes into the uses of some of the most common statistical tests and discusses some of the limitations of those tests, i.e. Chi-square using

Contingency Tables (Test of Independence), t-Test (Independent, Paired, and One Sample), One-Way ANOVA, Correlation, and Simple Linear Regression.

The focus of this guide will be the typical statistical analysis tools that may be useful for the novice or beginning researcher. Only a subset of the tools currently available in JASP will be covered. The guide does not include all of the tools and features available within the JASP application. The ones that were viewed as most common and readily available to the novice researcher are included.

The JASP application supports both Frequentist and Bayesian procedures. This guide will focus on the Frequentist methods. Discussions of both parametric and non-parametric methods are presented when applicable.

The sample windows and output tables shown in this guide were mainly created from JASP 0.18.3

The Philosophy Behind This Book and the Open-Source Community

This book began as my own attempt to find a practical way to teach introductory statistical analysis to students in the field of social sciences.

So began my search for an alternative that would be useful in learning basic analysis skills and capable of performing basic statistical analysis tests. This brought me to JASP. Developed at the University of Amsterdam, this powerful software package is effective and easy to use. Another key feature of the open-source group is that the software is distributed free of charge.

This guide is not intended to be a course on statistics or the mathematics behind statistical analysis. With the advent of statistical analysis applications anyone with a computer can run statistical analysis on any dataset. The intention of this guide is to provide the novice researcher with a step-by-step guide to using these powerful analysis tools and the confidence to interpret results tables in order to guide their own research.

Notes about the data

Data shown in this guide are from the JASP Data Library. Specific data types will be used to show the steps and procedures for various analysis methods; i.e. t-Test, ANOVA, Correlation, etc. This sample data should not be used to make assumptions or claims about the populations that they represent.

Chapter 2
The Language of Statistical Research

Why use statistics in Social Science research?

One of the assumptions made about quantitative research methods is that they merely deal with numbers. And let's face it, to many of us numbers are quite boring. A well-constructed data table or beautifully drawn graph does not capture the imagination of most readers. But appropriately used quantitative methods can uncover subtle differences, point out inconsistencies, or bring up more questions that beg to be answered.

In short, thoughtful quantitative methods can help guide and shape the qualitative story. This union of rich narratives and statistical evidence is at the heart of any good mixed methods study. The researcher uses the data to guide the narrative. Together these methods can reveal a more complete and complex account of the topic.

Statistical research has its own language. It is important that we understand the terms being used since these terms are how statistics can be clearly communicated. These terms include Categorical and Continuous data, Assumptions, p-values, statical significance, effect size, confidence interval, and many more. In this chapter we will focus on the key terminology that you will need to begin your statical journey.

What is Continuous and Categorical Data?

Within statistical analysis we often talk about data as being either continuous or categorical. This distinction is important since it guides us towards appropriate methods that are used for each kind of data set. Depending on the kind of data you have there are specific statistical techniques available for you to use with that data.

Continuous data can be thought of as "scaled data". The numbers may have been obtained from some sort of assessment or from some counting activity. A common example of continuous data is test scores.

Other examples of continuous data include;
- The time it takes to complete a task;
- A student's test scores;
- Number of hours that you study;
- The weight or height of a 2nd grade student.

All of these examples can be thought of as rational numbers. For those of us who have not been in an Algebra class for a number of years, rational numbers can be represented as fractions, which in turn can be represented as decimals. Rational numbers can still be represented as whole numbers as well.

A subset of this sort of data can be called discrete data, sometimes referred to as interval data. Discrete data is obtained from counting things. They are represented by whole numbers. It is important to note that when thinking about interval data, each point is an "equal distance" from one another. Imagine putting this data on a number line and the data is only plotted at the whole numbers. Some examples of discreet numbers include;
- The number of courses a student takes each year;
- The number of people living in a household;
- The number of languages spoken by someone;
- The number of turns taken by an individual.

Categorical data is another type of important statistical data, and one that is often used in social science research. As the name implies, categorical data is comprised of categories or the names of things that we are interested in studying. In working with statistical methods, we often transform the names of our categories into numbers so it can be analyzed using some software application.

An example of this process is when we collect information about a student's favorite class. We may be interested in whether or not students prefer Biology,

Chemistry, Geology, Algebra, Calculus, or Statistics. We may convert this data into numbers for analysis.

Favorite Class	Code
Biology	1
Chemistry	2
Geology	3
Algebra	4
Calculus	5
Statistics	6

Favorite Class Code Book

In the above example the numbers assigned to the categories do not signify any differences or order in the classes. The numbers used here are **"nominal"** or used to represent names.

Another example of categorical data could be the grade level of a high school student. In this case we may be interested in high school freshmen, sophomores, juniors, and seniors. Assigning a numerical label to these categories may make our analysis simpler.

Grade Level	Code
Freshman	1
Sophomore	2
Junior	3
Senior	4

In this example, again the numbers are just representing the names of the high school level, however they do have an order. "Freshman" comes prior to "Sophomore", which is prior to "Junior", and also "Senior". This sort of categorical data can be described as **ordinal**, or representing an order. Even though we can think of these terms having a specific order, they could not be plotted on a number line and have **equal distance** from one another. Order has meaning but distance does not have any meaning with the numbers used.

It is important to recognize the sort of data that is being used in the research analysis process. A researcher should ask;

- Does my data represent information that is continuous (a rational number) or is it categorical (names and labels)?
- Does this represent test scores or evaluations?
- Does this data represent something that has been counted?
- Is the interval between the data points a regular, measured interval?
- Does this data represent the names of something?

- Do the data points represent the order of objects?
- Are the data points opinions?

Depending on whether a researcher is using categorical or continuous data, there are specific statistical methods available. This guide will explore some of the most common statistical methods in social science research and the data associated with the method.

Parametric versus Non-Parametric Data

Our data can also be classified as either parametric or nonparametric. This term refers to the distribution of data points. Parametric data will have a "normal distribution" that is generally shaped like the typical bell curve. Non-parametric data does not have this normal distribution curve.

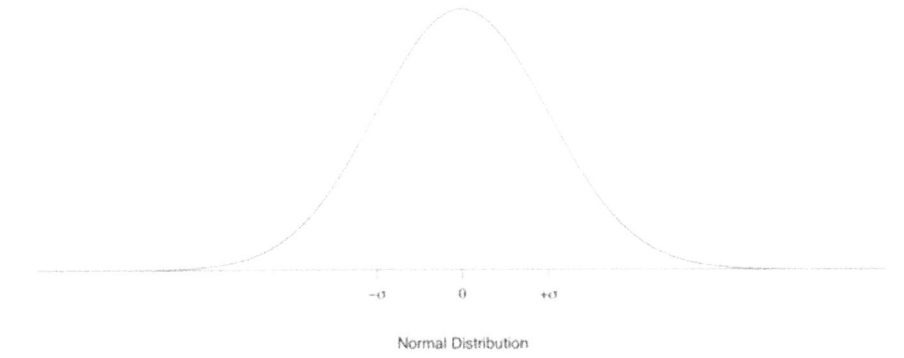

Normal Distribution Curve of parametric data

When parametric data is plotted in a histogram, the resulting graph will generally have a normal distribution shape.

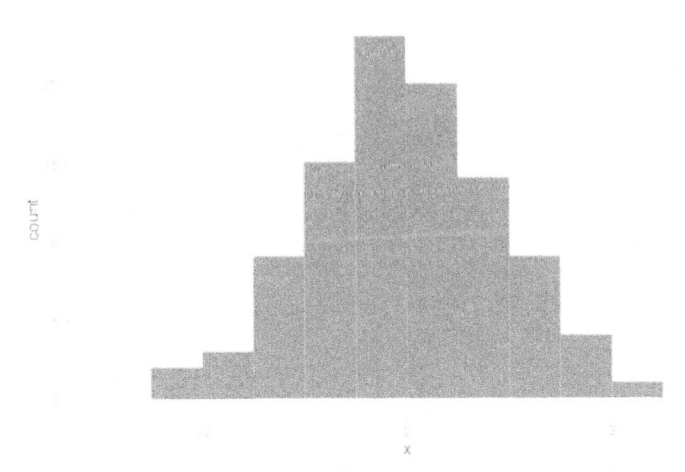

By Visnut - Own work, CC BY-SA 4.0, https://commons.wikimedia.org/w/index.php?curid=36192738

When non-parametric data is plotted in a histogram, the resulting graph will not have the normal distribution shape.

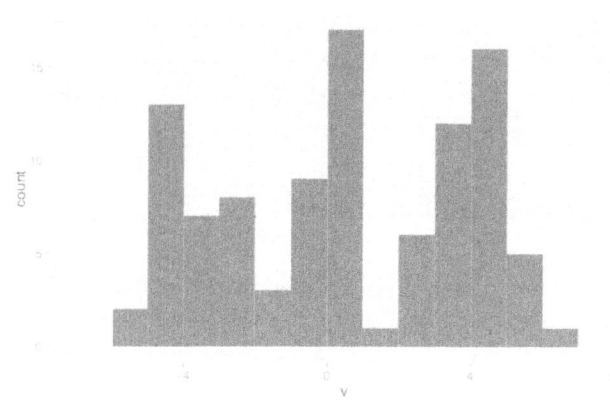

By Visnut - Own work, CC BY-SA 4.0, https://commons.wikimedia.org/w/index.php?curid=36192678

Depending on the distribution of your data, various statistical analysis techniques are available to use. Some methods are designed for parametric data while other methods are better suited for non-parametric data distributions.

So why does determining if the data is parametric or not matter? If you took a statistics course in high school, you may have calculated the results using an equation. The equation used for parametric data and non-parametric data is different. For example, below are the equations for the Independent Samples t-Test, a method to analyze the difference of two means.

$$t = \frac{\bar{X}_1 - \bar{X}_2}{s_p \sqrt{\frac{2}{n}}}$$

Parametric Equation

$$t = \frac{\Delta \bar{X}}{s_{\Delta \bar{X}}} = \frac{\bar{X}_1 - \bar{X}_2}{\sqrt{s_{\bar{X}_1}^2 + s_{\bar{X}_2}^2}}$$

Nonparametric Equation

We can see that there are some differences in the equations as well as similarities. The differences are to account for differences in the distribution and variance in the data. In determining if we should use the parametric or nonparametric version of these equations, certain statistical assumptions about the data must be examined.

Statistical Assumptions

The mathematics behind most statistical analysis are based on certain assumptions about the data. These assumptions allow the results to "work" across a wide array of scenarios, while still performing reliably and providing results that accurately describe the statistical model.

Parametric Tests: Assumes that the data follows a specific distribution, typically a normal (bell-shaped) distribution. They require numerical data and are best suited for large samples. Parametric tests are more precise under these conditions but can be sensitive to outliers.

Non-Parametric Tests: Does not assume a specific distribution of the data. They are more flexible, able to handle various types of data including ordinal, nominal, and non-normally distributed numerical data. Non-parametric tests are particularly useful for smaller samples and are more robust against outliers.

Two of the most common assumptions are concerned with the Normality of the data and its Homogeneity.

Normality is used to determine if a data set is well-modeled by a normal distribution and to compute how likely it is for a random variable within the data to be normally distributed.

Data that shows normal distribution will look very close to the classical bell-curve graph. A normal distribution is a way to describe how data points are spread out. It looks like a bell curve, which is highest in the middle and tapers off evenly on both sides. The middle point of the curve is the average (mean) of all the data points. This is also where the median and mode are located. The curve is perfectly symmetrical. This means the left side is a mirror image of the right side. So, a normal distribution is just a way to describe data that clusters around a central value with a predictable spread and shape.

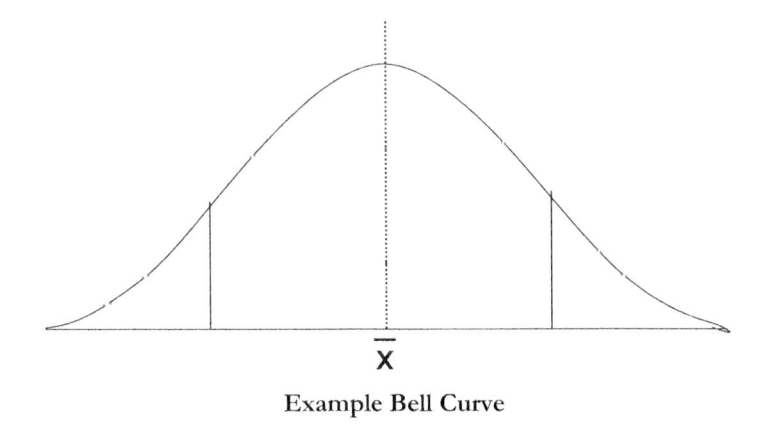

Example Bell Curve

Real world data is often quite messy and rarely conforms to this perfectly shaped distribution. The goal of **normality** is not to have data that mirrors the bell curve but to have our data approximate this distribution curve as closely as possible.

Quantitative Analysis

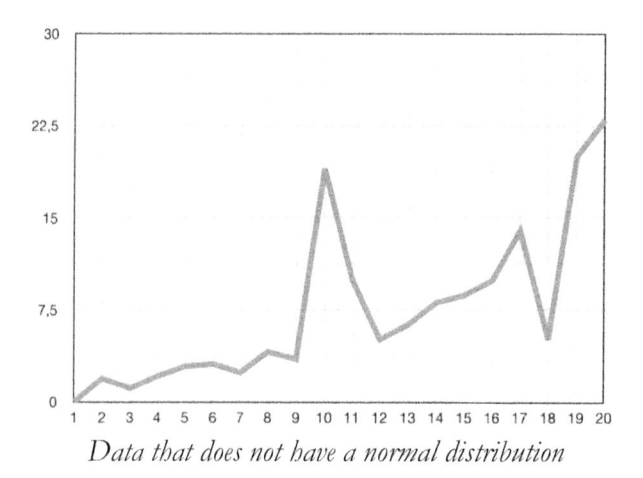

Data that does not have a normal distribution

Homogeneity refers to the uniformity or sameness within the data or between datasets. A dataset is considered homogeneous if the elements have similar mathematical characteristics.

Homogeneity assumes that the data of our sample populations have equal variation, or equal enough that when the expected and observed variances are graphed on a scatterplot, they would form something that resembles a line.

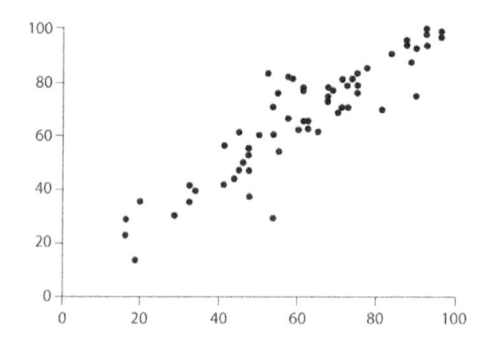

Example Variance Between Two Samples

We should keep in mind that both Normality and Homogeneity are assumptions in the statistical models, but these are not requirements. In the end it is up to the researcher to use good judgment when considering the statistical assumptions. A novice researcher should adhere to these basic assumptions as closely as possible.

Chapter 3
Frequentist Statistical Analysis

P-Value

What is a P-value?

In statistical analysis the way we measure the significance of any given test is with the P-value. This value indicates the probability of obtaining the same statistical result by chance. Our calculated p-values are compared against some predetermined significance level. The most common significance levels are the 95% significance level, represented by a p-value of 0.05, and the 99% significance level, represented by a p-value of 0.01. A significance level of 95%, or 0.05, indicates that we are accepting the risk of being wrong 1 out of every 20 times. A significance level of 99%, or 0.01, indicates that we risk being wrong only 1 out of every 100 times.

The most common significance level used in the Social Sciences is 95%, so we are looking for p-values < 0.05 in our test results to be considered statistically significant.

However, often times in statistical analysis we are not looking to prove our test hypothesis with the p-value. We are often trying to reject the Null Hypothesis.

Confidence Intervals (CI)

Much of inferential statistics is based on measurements and manipulations of the means. When we have sample data, the measures of central tendency, such as mean, median, and mode, are very simple to calculate and compare. When these measures are compared across categories, factors, or groupings we begin to find differences in their means.

Often we take sample data to represent some larger population. We can calculate the sample mean with certainty but the true mean of the population being represented cannot be known for certain through the sample data. This is when the confidence intervals come into consideration.

The confidence interval is a calculated range of values for the true mean. We can know with a certain amount of "confidence", typically at the 95% confidence level, that the true mean will fall within the specified confidence interval, or range.

This is similar to when a poll reports the percentage of people for or against the topic. The percentage is typically followed by a "plus or minus" statement.

The larger the confidence interval, the less certain we are about the results. For example, a poll stating that their sample results showed that 80% of people like stats may not be very useful if the confidence interval for the population is between 60% to 100%. This is a pretty wide margin for error.

We may find that the mean of our sample is 52.65 for some measure. The calculated confidence interval could be from 51.34 to 53.95 for the general population. Therefore, given that the sample mean is 52.65, we can state with 95% confidence that the true mean lies somewhere between 51.34 and 53.95 for the population.

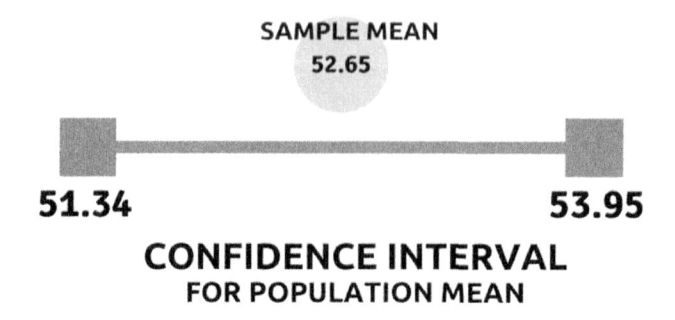

SAMPLE MEAN
52.65

51.34 **53.95**

CONFIDENCE INTERVAL
FOR POPULATION MEAN

What is the Null Hypothesis?

In statistical testing the results are always comparing two competing hypotheses. The null hypothesis tells us that whatever phenomenon we were observing had no or very little differences. On the other hand, we have the alternative, or researcher's hypothesis. This is the hypothesis that we are rooting for, the one that we want to accept in many cases. It is the result we often want to find since it indicates that there are associations and relationships between populations or conditions. Then we can take that next step to explain or examine them more closely.

We write these hypotheses in a specific way. For example;

- Null hypothesis: H_0 You will not find this guide useful.
- Alternative hypothesis: H_1 You will find this guide very useful.

When we perform a statistical test, the p-value helps determine the significance of the test and the validity of the claim being made. The claim that is always "on trial" here is the null hypothesis. When the p-value is found to be statistically significant ($p < 0.05$), or that it is highly statistically significant ($p < 0.01$), then we can conclude that the relationships or associations found in the observed data are very unlikely to occur by chance if the null hypothesis is true. Therefore, the researcher can "reject the null hypothesis". If you reject the null hypothesis, then the alternative hypothesis must be accepted. And this is often what we want as researchers.

The only question that the p-value addresses is whether or not the experiment or data provides enough evidence to reasonably reject null hypothesis. The p-value or calculated probability is the estimated probability of rejecting the null hypothesis of a study question when that null hypothesis is true. In other words, it measures the probability that you will be wrong in rejecting the null hypothesis. And all of this is decided based on our predetermined significance level, in most cases the 95% level or $p < 0.05$.

Let's look at an example. Suppose your school purchases a SAT Prep curriculum in the hopes that this will raise the SAT test scores of your students. Some students are enrolled in the prep course while others are not enrolled in the prep course. At the end of the course all your students take the SAT test and their resulting test scores are compared.

In this example our null hypothesis would be that "the SAT prep curriculum had no impact on student test scores". This result would be bad news considering how much time, effort, and money was invested in the test prep. The alternative hypothesis is that the prep curriculum did have an impact on the test scores, and hopefully the impact was to raise those scores. Our predetermined significance level is 95%. After using a statistical test suppose that we find a p-value of 0.02, which is indeed less than 0.05. We can reject the null hypothesis. Now that we have rejected the null hypothesis the only other option is to accept the alternative hypothesis, specifically that the scores are significantly different.

- Null hypothesis: H_0 The SAT prep curriculum had no impact on student test scores.
- Alternative hypothesis: H_1 The SAT prep curriculum had an impact on student test scores.

This result does NOT imply a "meaningful" or "important" difference in the data. That conclusion is for you to decide when considering the real-world relevance of your result. So again, statistical analysis is not the end point in research, but a meaningful beginning point to help the researcher identify important and fruitful directions suggested by the data.

It has been suggested that the idea of "rejecting the null hypothesis" has very little meaning for social science research. The null hypothesis always states that there are "no differences" to be found within your data. Can we really find NO DIFFERENCES in the data? Are the results that we find between two groups ever going to be identical to one another?

The practical answer to these questions is "No". There will always be differences present in our data. What we are really asking is whether or not those differences have any statistical significance. As we discussed previously, our statistical tests are aimed at producing the p-value that indicates the likelihood of having the differences occur purely by chance. And the significance level of $p = 0.05$ is just an agreed upon value among many social scientists as the acceptable level to consider as statistically significant.

And to find that the differences within the data are statistically significant may just be a factor of having a large enough sample size to make those differences meaningful.

A small p-value (typically ≤ 0.05) indicates strong evidence against the null hypothesis, so you reject the null hypothesis. A large p-value (> 0.05) indicates weak evidence against the null hypothesis, so you fail to reject the null hypothesis. P-values very close to the cutoff (0.05) are considered to be marginal so you could go either way. But keep in mind that the choice of significance levels is arbitrary. We have selected a significance level of 95% because of the conventions used in most Social Science research. I could have easily selected a significance level of 80%, but then no one would take my results very seriously.

Relying on the p-value alone can give you a false sense of security. The p-value is also very sensitive to sample size. If a given sample size yields a p-value that is close to the significance level, increasing the sample size can often shift the p-value in a favorable direction, i.e. make the resulting value smaller.

So how can we use p-values and have a sense of the magnitude of the differences? This is where Effect Size can help.

Effect Size

Whereas statistical tests of significance tell us the likelihood that experimental results differ from chance expectations, effect-size measurements tell us the relative magnitude of those differences found within the data. Effect sizes are especially important because they allow us to compare the magnitude of results from one population or sample to the next.

Effect size is not as sensitive to sample size since it relies on standard deviation in the calculations. Effect size also allows us to move beyond the simple question of "does this work or not?" or "is there a difference or not?", but allows us to ask the question "how well does some intervention work within the given context?"

Let's take a look at an example that could, and has happened, to many of us when conducting statistical analysis. When we compare two data sets, perhaps we are looking at SAT assessment scores between a group of students who enrolled in a SAT prep course and another group of students who did not enroll in the prep course.

Suppose that the statistical test revealed a p-value of 0.057. We should report that there is no statistical difference between the group of test takers enrolled in the prep course and those who were not enrolled in the course. But what if the calculated p-value was 0.044. Does this mean that the prep course is effective? Here is where the effect size could provide more information. In this example suppose the p-vales was 0.047 and the effect size was calculated to be very small. Then the conclusion would be that even though there is a statistical difference in the data, the effect size does not warrant much consideration.

Another way to think about the effect size is to describe it has the "visible" differences that we find in the data. Effect size is described as small, medium, or large effect sizes.

Suppose we had a room filled with nineth grade students and eighth grade students. It is likely that the difference in height between the two groups is statistically significant. But what if you were going to visually sort them into the two groups? Chances are you would have some nineth graders in the correct group, some eighth graders in the correct group, and a lot of students that you would just have to guess.

This is an example of a **small effect size**.

Let's fill that room again. This time we have a group of nineth graders and a group of seventh graders. Their height differences are still statistically significant. When you sort them into the two groups, you can identify most of the nineth graders and most of the seventh graders. There are still some that you are just not certain about which group to put them.

This is an example of a **medium effect size**.

Ok, one more room full of students. This time we filled it with nineth graders and sixth graders. Their difference in height is statistically significant. When we go to sort them, the differences are so obvious that we get almost all of them into the correct groups.

This is an example of a **large effect size**.

So here is the bottom-line. The p-value calculation will help us decide if a difference or association has some significance that should be explored further. The effect size will give us a sense of the magnitude of any differences to help us decide if those differences have any practical meaning and are worth exploring.

Both the p-value and the effect size can be used to assist the researcher in making meaningful judgments about the differences found within our data.

Determining the Magnitude of Effect Size

Once we have calculated the effect size value we must determine if this value represents a small, medium, or large effect. Jacob Cohen (1988) suggested various effect size calculations and magnitudes in his text *Statistical Power Analysis for the Behavioral Sciences*.

The values in the effect size magnitude chart can be thought of as a range of values with the numbers in each column representing the midpoint of that particular range. For example, the effect size chart for Phi suggests a small, medium, and large effect size for the values of 0.1, 0.3, and 0.5 respectively. We could think of these as ranges with the small effect for Phi ranging from 0.0 to approximately 0.2, the medium effect size ranging from approximately 0.2 to 0.4, and the large effect size ranging from approximately 0.4 and higher.

Suggested Effect Size Magnitude Chart

Effect Size Calculation	Statistics Test	Small Effect	Medium Effect	Large Effect
Phi or Cramer's Phi	Chi Squared	0.1	0.3	0.5
Cohen's d	t-Test (Paired & Independent)	0.2	0.5	0.8
Partial Eta Squared	ANOVA	0.01	0.06	0.14
r	Correlation	0.1	0.3	0.5

Values from Cohen (1988) Statistical Power Analysis for the Behavioral Sciences

We can now take p-values and effect size into account when determining the strength of our evidence for either the Alternative Hypothesis (H_1) or the Null Hypothesis (H_0).

The table below was suggested by Wetzels et al (2011).

Statistic	Interpretation
P-value	
< 0.001	Decisive evidence against H_0
0.001 – 0.01	Substantive evidence against H_0
0.01 – 0.05	Positive evidence against H_0
> 0.05	No evidence against H_0
Effect Size (Cohen's d)	
< 0.2	Small effect size
0.2 -0.5	Small to medium effect size
0.5 – 0.8	Medium to large effect size
> 0.8	Large to very large effect size

Chapter 4
Getting Started with JASP

Preparing the Data and Making Decisions

Now that we have data collected from our study it is time to perform some analysis to address the research questions posed. One of the first choices made has to do with entering your data into an application so that you can actually do the analysis. Depending on the kind of data you have collected there are many choices available.

We will focus on using continuous and categorical data sets with the JASP statistical analysis application.

Thinking about Data

Whether you plan to perform data entry into a spreadsheet first or not, you will need to create a codebook for your data. The codebook is used as a planning tool and a quick reference guide to your data. There are some questions that must be addressed prior to data entry.

Continuous Data
- How large is your data set?
- Will all the data be manually entered into the spreadsheet?
- How many decimal places are required for your data?

- How will you "name" the data for easy reference?
- Are there any outliers in the data?
- How will you handle outliers?

Categorical Data
- What are the value names for each data item?
- How will you represent each value name with an integer value?
- Is your data nominal or ordinal? How will this guide the decision for selecting values?

With any categorical data, we begin by converting the labels, such as socioeconomic status or school, type, into numerical values that can be manipulated in the analysis application.

Some of the data could be nominal in nature. There is not any order to the labels and an order should not be implied from the values. For example, the value for school type has been listed "public, private, and charter" with values of "1, 2, and 3" assigned respectively. This does not imply the "public" is first, "private" is second, and "charter" is third. These labels could have been placed in any order and assigned any value.

On the other hand if your data had involved grade level or degrees attained, then we might be able to assign values based on an order, so this would represent ordinal data; a group with some defined order.

Data in JASP

JASP is able to handle and distinguish between four variables, or data types:

1. Nominal Text, also known as String data.
2. Nominal Categorical data representing "names".
3. Ordinal Categorical data representing "names in an order".
4. Continuous real numbers such as integers, whole numbers, decimals.

Nominal Text variables are typically used to identify aspects of the data that will not be part of the statistical analysis. This data merely contains descriptions, key words, or some other type of text information.

Nominal Categorical variables are categorical variables that are represented by numeric values. For example, a variable "Courses" may have levels "0" and "1" representing Math courses and Science courses respectively. Even though these are numbers, they do not imply an order, and the distance between them is not meaningful.

Ordinal Categorical variables are categorical variables with an inherent order. The ordinal variables could represent some sort of order such as a grade level with 1 = Freshman, 2 = Sophomore, 3 = Junior, and 4 = Senior. Note that the distance between the numbers is not meaningful. JASP assumes that all ordinal variables have been assigned numeric values.

Continuous variables are variables with values that allow a meaningful comparison of distance. Examples include money, distance, and test scores. Often we make the assumption that rubric scores are continuous variables since the rubric levels of 1, 2, 3, and 4 should represent some meaningful difference between them.

Variable types in JASP are "enforced". This means that JASP will not allow performing a categorical variable analysis using continuous data or performing continuous variable calculations with categorical (nominal and ordinal) data.

Using .SAV in JASP

The JASP statistical application is able to natively use ".sav" file formats. This means that files created within SPSS, or any other compatible application can be easily opened with JASP without having to convert the file.

Click on the "File" icon from the top left corner of the screen, then use the dialogue windows to select the .sav data file from your computer.

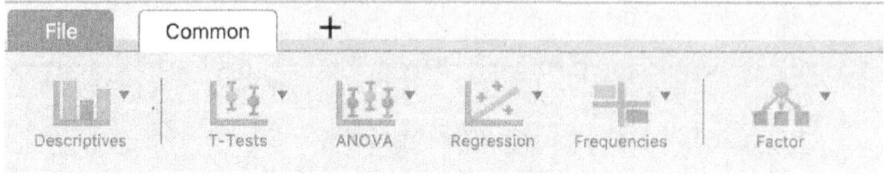

JASP Open File icon

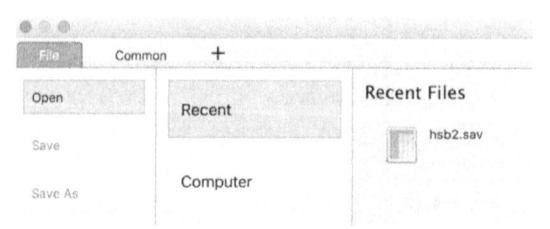

JASP Open Dialogue Box

The file will open with the variable names and data.

A JASP Guide: Foundational Methods

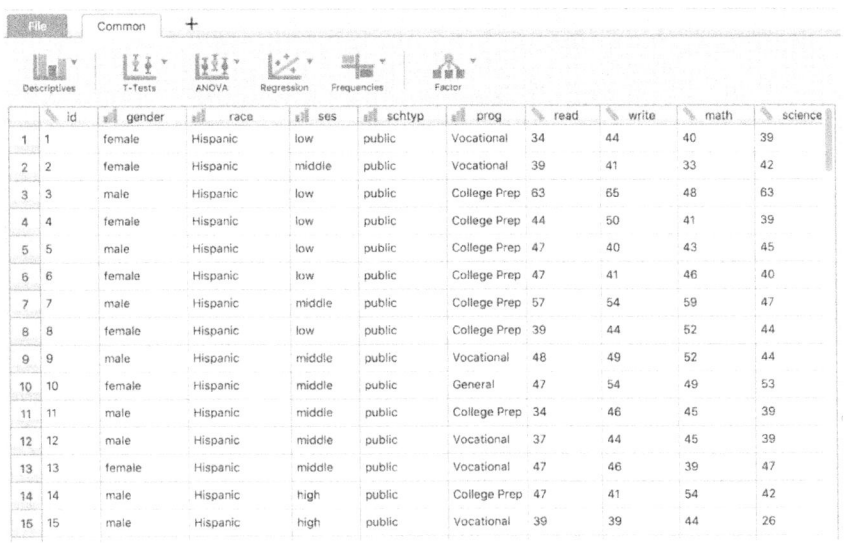

JASP Data View window with Data

JASP can also open files in other formats such as .csv (comma-separated values), .txt (plain text), .sav (IBM's SPSS), and .ods (OpenDocument Spreadsheet).

Spreadsheets in JASP (.osd & .csv)

Setting Up the Spreadsheet (.osd)

JASP is able to use OpenDocument Spreadsheets (.ods). Spreadsheet files need to have a header row that contains names for each of the columns or variables. Missing values can either just be missing (i.e., an empty cell) or be denoted by "Nan", "." (period), or " " (space).

Getting the spreadsheet setup and the data entered is a simple process. There are a few key points to keep in mind:

- In the spreadsheet, the columns contain each variable or data type and the rows represent each case in the study. This is similar to the way JASP displays the data.
- The first row of the spreadsheet should be the variable names with row 2 containing the first data. Variable names should be short, but meaningful to you.
- Categorical data must be entered as its numerical value and not the name. The codebook you created will come in handy for this process.
- Enter all the data.

Quantitative Analysis

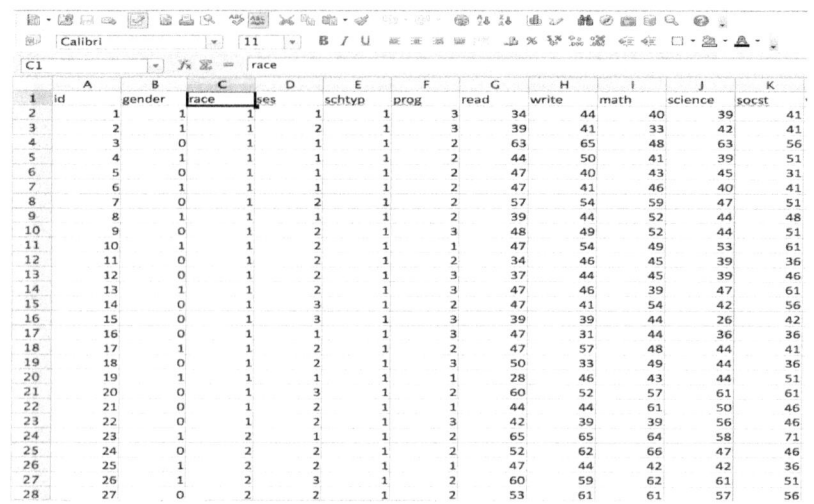

OpenOffice Spreadsheet with data labels shown as numerical values vice names

Opening the Spreadsheet (.ods)

To open the .ods file in JASP, click on the File tab at the top of the screen. Using the dialogue box, navigate to the .ods file to select and open the file. JASP will use the entered data to determine the type of data in each column, i.e. Nominal, Ordinal, or Continuous. The data type will be represented by an icon next to the column header.

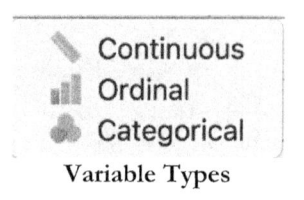

Variable Types

The ruler icon represents Continuous data, the bar graph icon represents Categorical Ordinal data, and the Venn Diagram icon represents Categorical Nominal data.

If JASP assigned an incorrect data type to your column, this can be corrected by clicking on the icon to activate a pull-down menu. The data type can be changed by selecting the desired type.

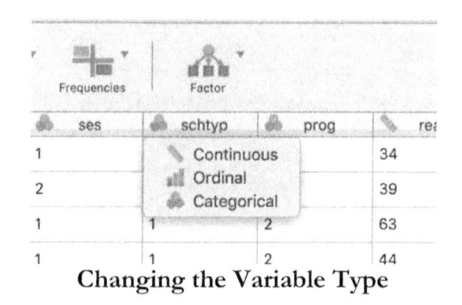

Changing the Variable Type

22

If the data type is Categorical, you can assign labels to the values by clicking on the column header. This will show the Label window. When the .ods file is opened by JASP, the values and the labels will initially be the same.

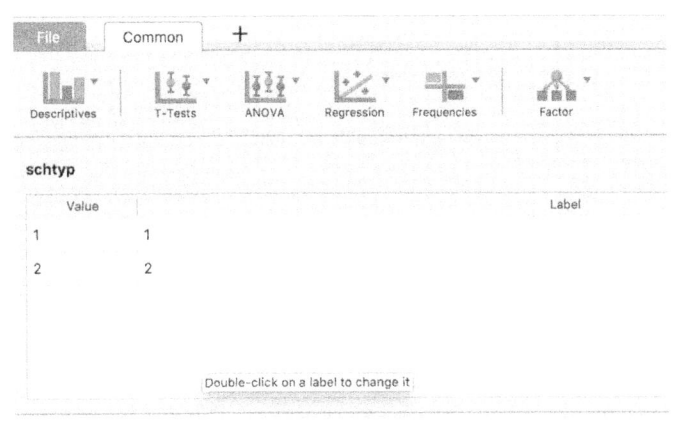

Value labels

To change the label, click in the Label field and enter the desired text.

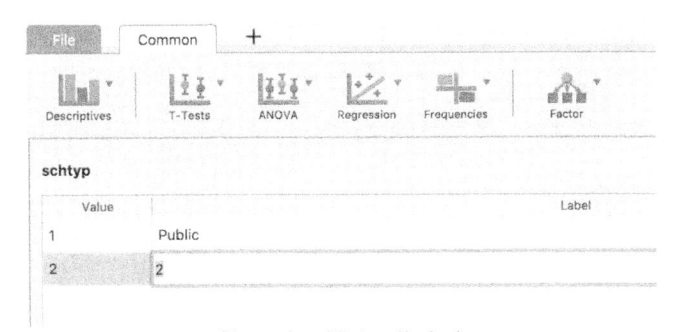

Changing Value Labels

Setting Up the Spreadsheet (.csv)

JASP is able to use Comma Separated Values(.csv) in the application. Spreadsheet files need to have a header row that contains names for each of the columns or variables. Missing values can either just be missing (i.e., an empty cell) or be denoted by "Nan", "." (period), or " " (space).

Getting the spreadsheet setup and the data entered is a simple process. There are a few key points to keep in mind:

- In the spreadsheet, the columns contain each variable or data type, and the rows represent each case in the study. This is similar to the way JASP displays the data.

Quantitative Analysis

- The first row of the spreadsheet should be the variable names with row 2 containing the first data. Variable names should be short, but meaningful to you.
- Categorical data must be entered as its numerical value and not the name. The codebook you created will come in handy for this process.
- Enter all the data.

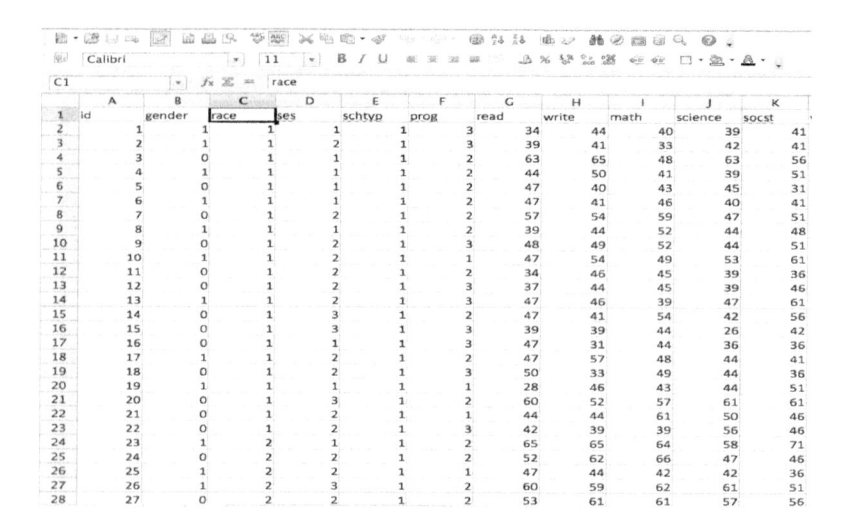

Spreadsheet with data labels shown as numerical values vice names

Opening the Spreadsheet (.csv)

To open the .csv file in JASP, click on the File tab at the top of the screen. Using the dialogue box, navigate to the .csv file to select and open the file. JASP will use the entered data to determine the type of data in each column, i.e. Nominal, Ordinal, or Continuous. The data type will be represented by an icon next to the column header.

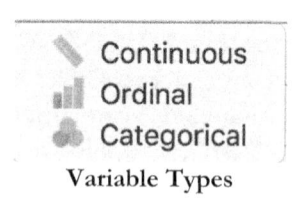

Variable Types

The ruler icon represents Continuous data, the bar graph icon represents Categorical Ordinal data, and the Venn Diagram icon represents Categorical Nominal data.

If JASP assigned an incorrect data type to your column, this can be corrected by clicking on the icon to activate a pull-down menu. The data type can be changed by selecting the desired type.

Changing Variable Types

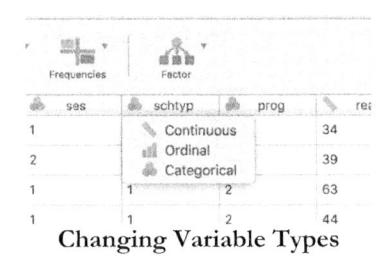

If the data type is Categorical, you can assign labels to the values by clicking on the column header. This will show the Label window. When the .csv file is opened by JASP, the values and the labels will initially be the same.

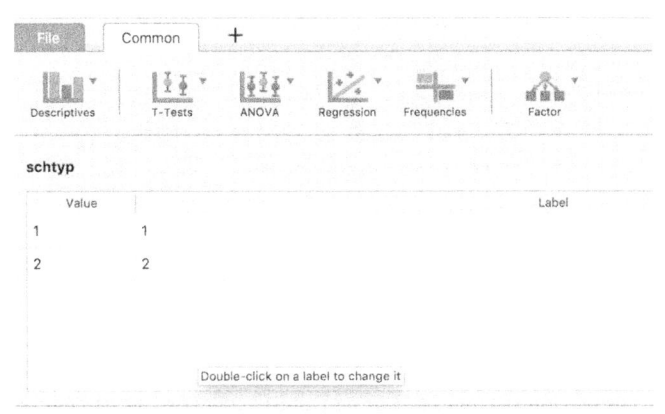

Variable Labels

To change the label, click in the Label field and enter the desired text.

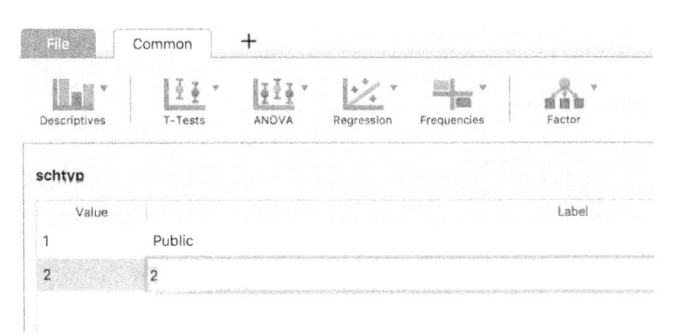

Changing Variable Labels

It should be noted that any changes made to the labels or data types in JASP will not affect the original .csv spreadsheet.

Creating .jasp File

Once a data file, either sav, ods or csv, is opened in JASP, it may be advantageous to save the information as a native ".jasp" file. The original file would be opened as described in the previous sections of this guide, any necessary changes made to the variable type, and the inclusion of any variable labels.

Click on the File tab and select the "Save As" command.

Save As Function

Next, click on the "Browse" button to select the folder that will contain the new file.

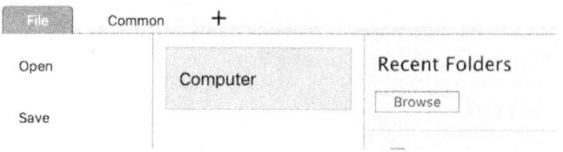

Browse Function

The advantage to saving a ".jasp" file for your analysis is that all the results tables, graphics, researcher inserted notes, etc. will be saved as part of the ".jasp" file, saving all of the analysis work.

Tutorials and Help

JASP comes with a very detailed guide that is built into the application. The guidance and examples are contained in the JASP Data Library. This library contains over 50 data sets to practice various statistical analysis techniques.

To access the Data Library, click on the File tab then click on Data Library from the menu choices.

Data Library Menu

To access a specific data set example, click on any of the folder icons under the Data Library's categories. You will see a list of example data sets that are appropriate to use for the statistical methods shown in the folder.

Here we have selected the "T-Test" folder. Listed are all the data sets for that folder with a brief description of the data that it contains.

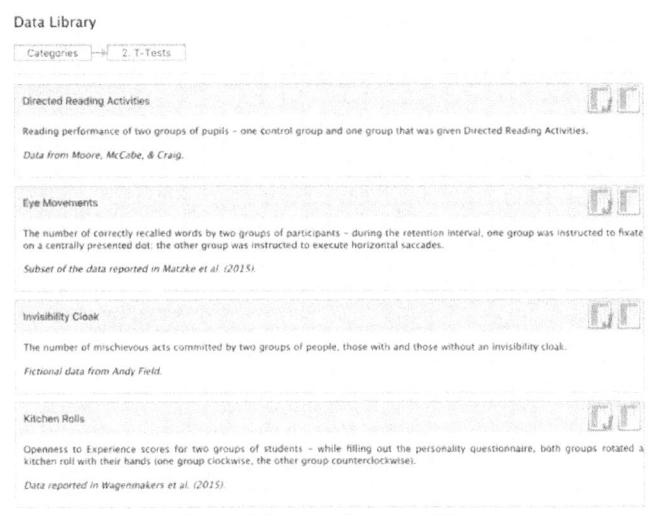

Data Library Sample Files

To open the data set, simply double click the file name. The data will load into JASP. Once the data is loaded into the JASP window, you will see the data in the left-hand window along with the results for the selected statistical analysis in the right-hand window.

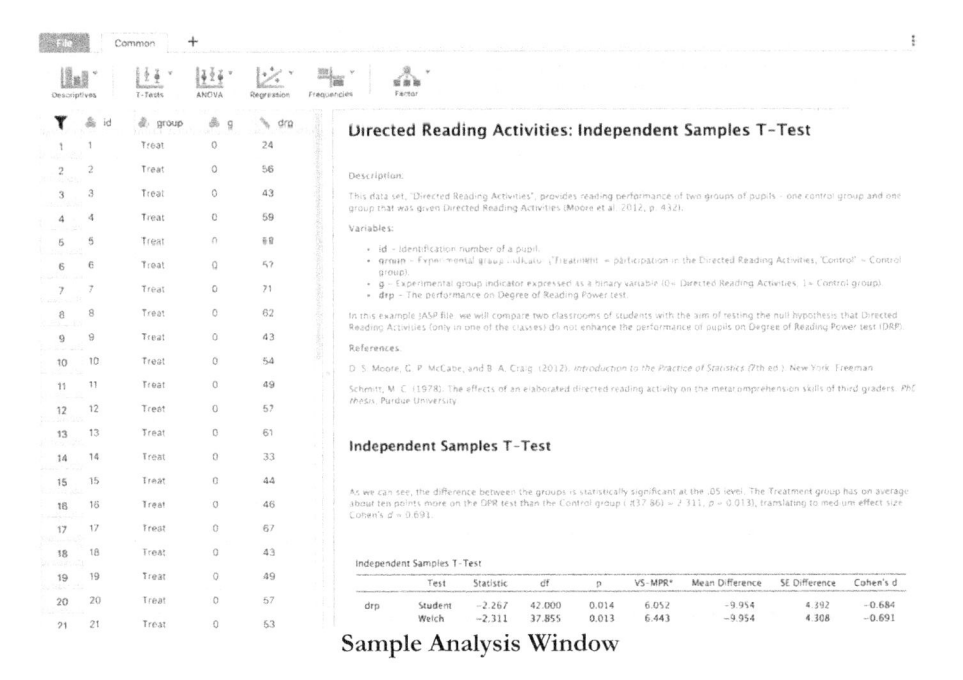

Sample Analysis Window

Quantitative Analysis

The results window will contain all the tables and output produced by the analysis; in this example we see the results for an Independent Samples T-Test. There will also be notes, shown as blue text, that explain the data and the results shown in each table.

Independent Samples T-Test ▼

As we can see, the difference between the groups is statistically significant at the .05 level. The Treatment group has on average about ten points more on the DPR test than the Control group ($t(37.86) = 2.311$, $p = 0.013$), translating to medium effect size: Cohen's $d = 0.691$.

Independent Samples T-Test

	Test	Statistic	df	p	VS-MPR*	Mean Difference	SE Difference	Cohen's d
drp	Student	−2.267	42.000	0.014	6.052	−9.954	4.392	−0.684
	Welch	−2.311	37.855	0.013	6.443	−9.954	4.308	−0.691

* Vovk-Sellke Maximum p-Ratio: Based on a two-sided p-value, the maximum possible odds in favor of H_1 over H_0 equals $1/(-e \, p \log(p))$ for $p \leq .37$ (Sellke, Bayarri, & Berger, 2001).
Note. For all tests, the alternative hypothesis specifies that group *Control* is less than group *Treat*.

Since the variance appears to be larger in the control group (see also the violin plot below), we consider the Welch version of the t-test; the Welch version does not assume that the variances in the two groups are equal.

Sample Analysis Window with Notes

You can follow the steps described in the results window to practice the analysis technique on your own.

Section II: Descriptive Statistics and Data Visualization

Chapter 5
Descriptive Statistics

What are descriptive statistics?

Descriptive statistics are used to characterize the data in order to make decisions about the nature, tendencies, and appropriate inferential statistics that can be used to analyze the data or to simply make initial analysis decisions. In descriptive statistics we look at various measures such as mean, median, mode, and standard deviations. The two main concerns of descriptive statistics are measures of central tendency (mean, median, mode) and spread (standard deviation and variance).

Creating Descriptive Statistics in JASP for Categorical Data

Categorical data is best described by exploring the frequencies within the data. The frequencies will display the percentages of each category within the data set. The following examples will use the Directed Reading Activities dataset in the Data Library. The "Directed Reading Activities" provides reading performance of two groups of pupils - one control group and one group that was given Directed Reading Activities. This data comes from Schmitt's PhD thesis at Purdue University (1978), entitled "The effects of an elaborated directed reading activity on the meta comprehension skills of third graders".

A JASP Guide: Foundational Methods

Open the Directed Reading Activity dataset from the JASP data Library
Data Library > Categories > t-Test > Directed Reading Activities

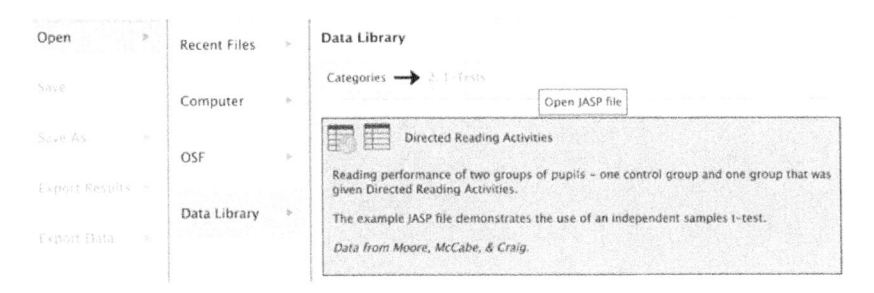

Some analysis results have already been completed in the Data Library. We will be creating some additional results tables.

Click on the Descriptives menu.

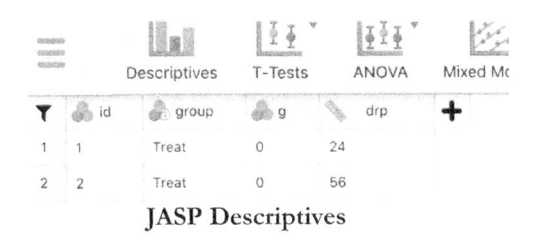

JASP Descriptives

There are four data points in this dataset.
- "id" has the data icon represents an id number assigned to each participant in the study.
- "group" with the icon is merely text data that provides the name for each group in the study.
- "g" with the icon is Categorical data that has assigned a numerical value to the group names so that raw data can be analyzed.
- "drp" with the is Continuous data representing the assessment scores of the students on the directed reading program assessment test.

Descriptive Statistics for Categorical (Nominal and Ordinal) Data

When considering Categorical data, it is often helpful to investigate that data from a descriptive standpoint. Here we are interested in frequencies, counts, comparisons between categories, etc.

The Descriptive Statistics' dialogue window, on the left side of the JASP window, allows us to select the measures and visualizations that are needed to get a clear sense of our data. As these measures are selected, the results will appear in the JASP window on the right side.

Quantitative Analysis

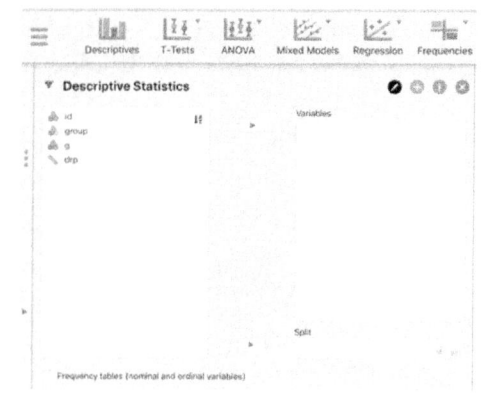

JASP Descriptive Statistics Dialogue Window

In our example, we are interested in the categorical variable the has data for the two groups; Directed Reading Activities group = 0 and the Control group = 1. In the data set, labels have not been given to these variables. To make reading the results table easier, you can add labels to this nominal data.

When you click on the name of the data in the header, a dialogue box will open so that you can enter labels for each numerical value used.

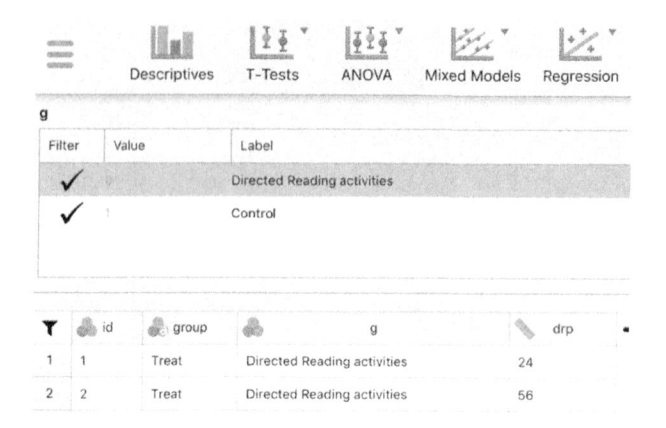

We can begin the analysis process by clicking on the Descriptives tab. This will activate the descriptive analysis settings.

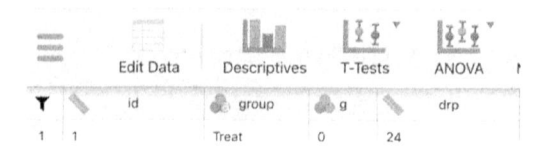

When the settings window is open, we can begin the analysis process. Begin by moving a Categorical item into the Variables window. This can be accomplished by either clicking and dragging the item or by selecting the item and clicking the arrow between the two boxes. Clicking on the label again will close the dialogue box.

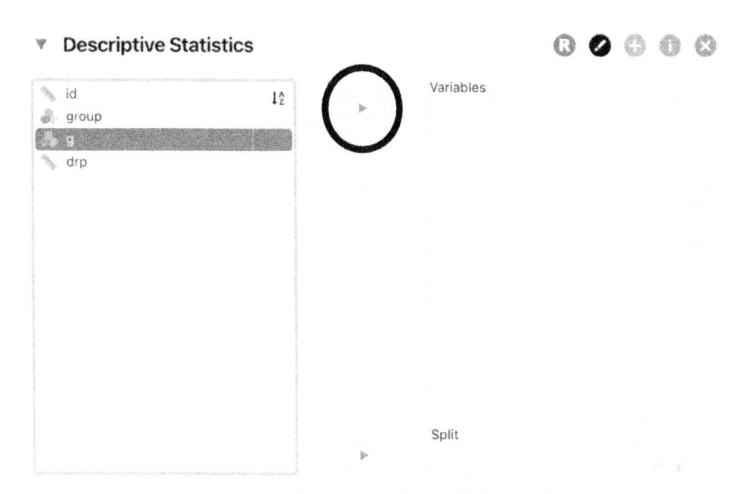

Descriptive Statistics for DRP activities

Once the Categorical data item is moved into the Variables box, the Descriptives results table will update with the new information. The next step will be considering which measures make sense for the data you are using.

When considering the analysis of categorical data, we often ignore the measures of central tendency and variation. Mean, median, and mode do not hold much meaning when the numerical values represent names and do not represent any actual numerical value. Likewise, standard deviation does not have much meaning for categorical data either.

For this analysis, we can skip the "Statistics" pull down menu.

▶ Statistics

Frequency tables and certain graphs provide the most useful information when considering categorical data.

We can move on to the Basic Plots settings to decide which graphical visualizations make sense for our data. In this case we will only be selecting Distribution Plots and Pie Charts for our Categorical data since this will provide us with useful information and visual representation about the category.

Quantitative Analysis

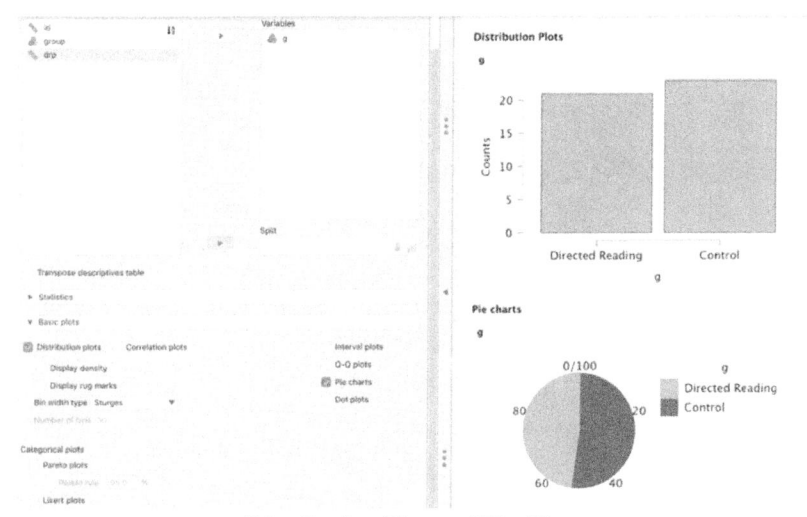

Distribution Plot and Pie Chart

If you need to go back and make changes to any of the previously selected settings, simply click in the output section of the Results window and the settings will be displayed in the left side window.

A Frequency table will give us some more numerical information about the categorical data. The table will provide a count for each label and the percentage of that label in the data. The Frequency table can be found in the Tables pull-down menu.

Open the pull-down menu and select "Frequency Tables".

Frequency Tables

Frequencies for g

g	Frequency	Percent	Valid Percent	Cumulative Percent
Directed Reading	21	47.727	47.727	47.727
Control	23	52.273	52.273	100.000
Missing	0	0.000		
Total	44	100.000		

Within the JASP Results window, we can include our own thoughts, notes, ideas, and points of interest about the data. For each output section of the Results window you will find a small pull-down arrow when the pointer hovers over the output.

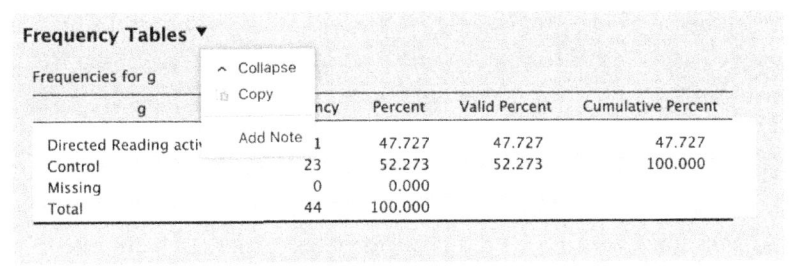

A JASP Guide: Foundational Methods

Frequency Tables ▼

Frequencies for g

g	Frequency	Percent	Valid Percent	Cumulative Percent
Directed Reading activities	21	47.727	47.727	47.727
Control	23	52.273	52.273	100.000
Missing	0	0.000		
Total	44	100.000		

(menu: Collapse, Copy, Add Note)

Frequencies Table

Clicking the arrow will bring up the dialogue menu to "Add Note". The researcher's note can then be entered into a new section above the output table.

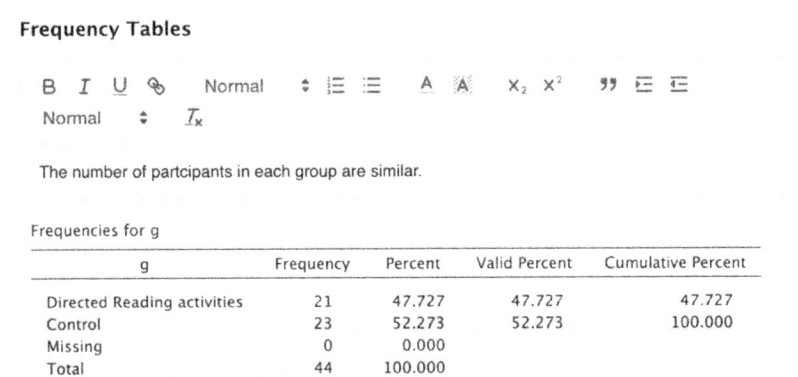

Frequency Tables

B I U ⚭   Normal ⇅ ≣ ≣ A 𝔸 X_2 x^2 ,, ⇥ ⇤
Normal ⇅ I_x

The number of partcipants in each group are similar.

Frequencies for g

g	Frequency	Percent	Valid Percent	Cumulative Percent
Directed Reading activities	21	47.727	47.727	47.727
Control	23	52.273	52.273	100.000
Missing	0	0.000		
Total	44	100.000		

Frequencies Table for the groups

One of the powerful features of JASP is that the output tables and graphics can easily be imported into a word processing document. The JASP Results section also displays the tables in APA format.

Use the same pull-down arrow, you can select "Copy" to place the table into your clipboard allowing it to be pasted into a different application or document.

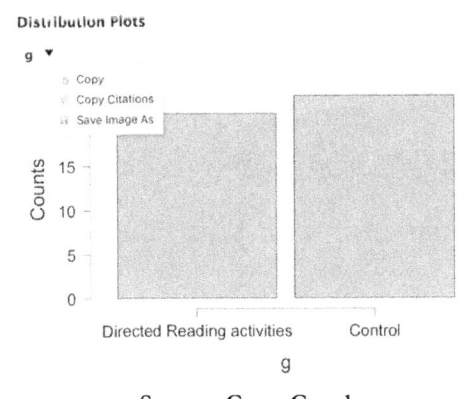

Distribution Plots

g ▼
 Copy
 Copy Citations
 Save Image As

(bar chart showing Counts on y-axis (0–15+) for Directed Reading activities and Control on x-axis labeled g)

Save or Copy Graphs

35

When the pull-down for graphs is selected, we are presented with the "Copy" option as well as a "Save Image As" option, allowing us to export the graph as a .png image.

Descriptive Statistics for Continuous Data

When considering Continuous data, i.e. measures and assessments, it is often helpful to investigate that data from a descriptive standpoint. These descriptive statistics should include frequencies, counts, mean, median, mode, standard deviation, etc. In general, with continuous data we are interested in the measures of central tendency and the variation or spread of the data.

The Descriptive Statistics dialogue window, on the left side of the JASP window, allows us to select the measures and visualizations that are needed to get a clear sense of our data.

As these measures are selected, the output will appear in the JASP Results window on the right side. In this example we are interested in the Directed Reading Power score (drp).

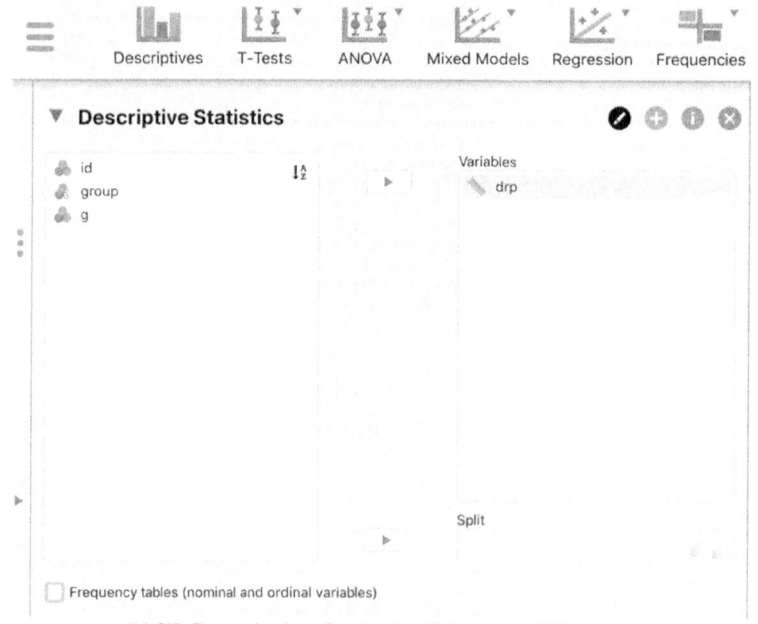

JASP Descriptive Statistics Dialogue Window

Begin by moving a Continuous item into the Variables window. This can be accomplished by either clicking and dragging the item or by selecting the item and clicking the arrow between the two boxes.

A JASP Guide: Foundational Methods

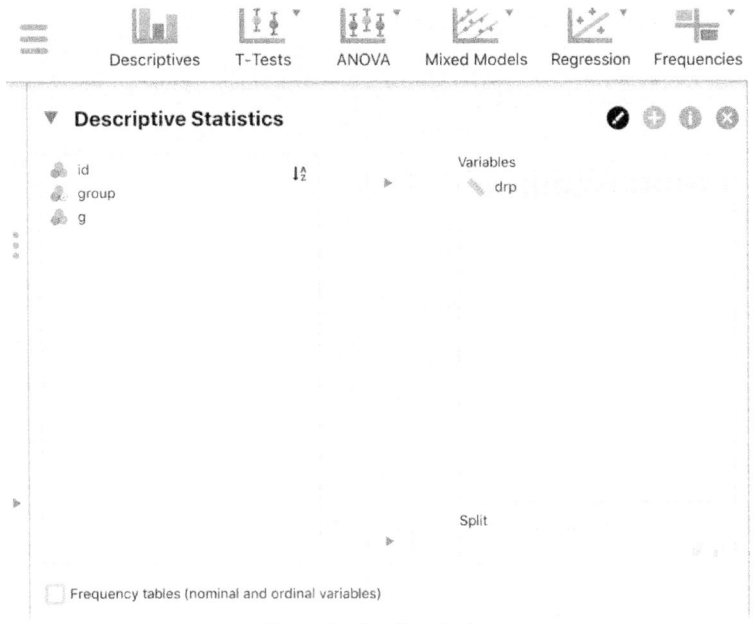

Descriptive Statistics

Once the Continuous data item is moved into the Variables box, the Descriptives results table will update with the new information. The next step will be considering which measures make sense for the data you are using.

Basic Descriptive Statistics

We can select settings from the "Statistics" section. In the case of our Continuous data, most of these settings will provide us with meaningful information as we examine the measures and begin to make sense of the data. As we select settings that are needed, the Descriptive Statistics table on the right-side window will automatically update.

Statistics Settings in JASP

37

Quantitative Analysis

If you need to go back and make changes to any of the previously selected settings, simply click in the output section of the Results window and the settings will be displayed in the left side window. Some of the more useful descriptive statistics are shown below in the settings window.

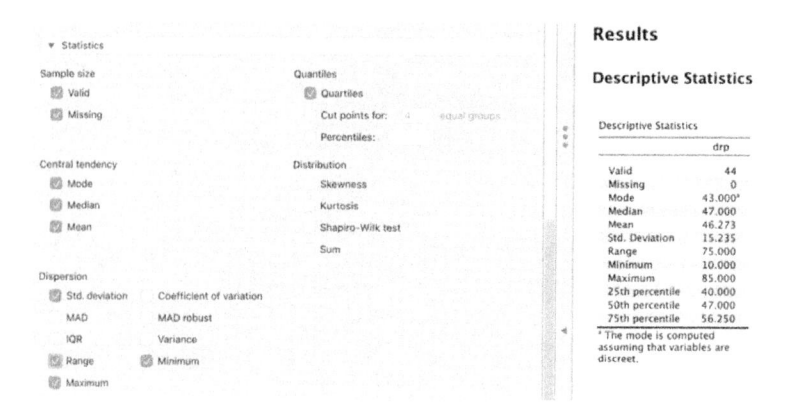

There are a few terms that may be useful;

Central Tendency
- **Mean** is the average of the numbers. Add up all the numbers, then divide by how many numbers there are.
- **Median** is the *"middle"* of a sorted list of numbers. To find the Median, place the numbers in value order and find the middle.
- **Mode** is the number which appears most often.

Dispersion/Variance
- **Range** is the difference between the lowest and highest values.
- **Minimum** refers to the smallest number in the data.
- **Maximum** refers to the largest number in the data.
- **Standard Deviation** (Std Dev column) gives a measure of the variation in our test scores from the mean. The scores can be described as 1 standard deviation from the mean, or 2 standard deviations from the mean, or 3 standard deviations from the mean. The standard deviations follow the 68-95-99 rule in statistics, in that 68% of the data falls within the first standard deviation, 95% of the data falls within the second standard deviation, and 99% of the data falls within the third standard deviation.

Standard Deviation Diagram

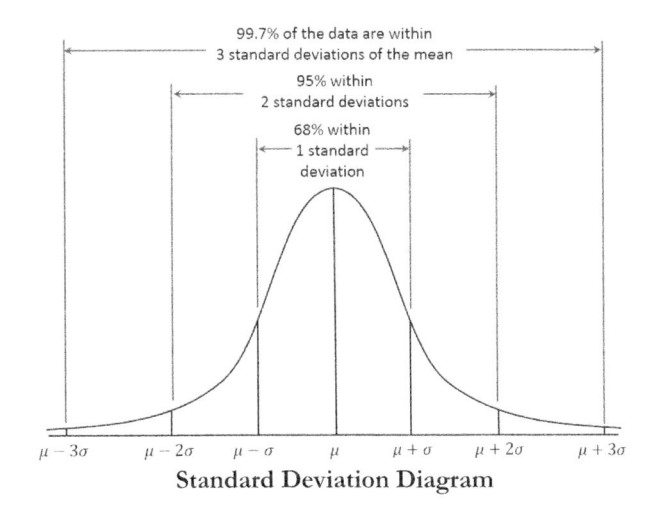

Distribution

- **Kurtosis** describes the "peakness" of the data. A kurtosis value of zero represents data that resembles a normally distributed data set. Positive values represent data with a **leptokurtic** distribution, or very high peaks, and negative values represent data with a **platykurtic** distribution, or one that is flatter.
- **Skewness** gives us information about the distribution of data from the mean. A skewness value of zero would have data evenly distributed and balanced around the mean. A positive skewness value indicates data weighted more heavily to the right of the mean and a negative skewness value indicates data weighted to the left of the mean.

Graphs and Visualizing Continuous Data

We can look at the **Basic Plots** settings to decide which graphical visualizations make sense for our data. In this case we will be selecting "Distribution Plots" for our Continuous data as well as the Dot plots to provide us with useful information.

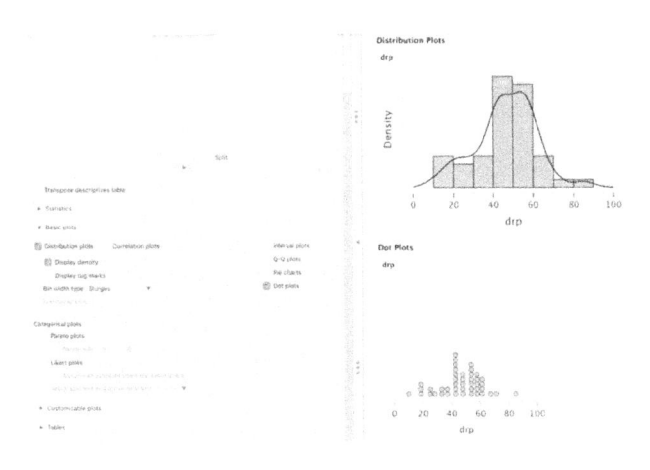

The Distribution plot will display a histogram of the data with a curve superimposed over the graph when you select the "Display density" checkbox. This curve will help us determine if the data has a "somewhat" normal distribution.

The Dot plot will create a simple scatterplot of the data with each data point represented as a plot. The dot plot will mirror the distribution graph with the individual dots allowing the researcher to judge how many data points are in each "bar" shown in the distribution plot.

The **Customizable Plots** tab will let us create a Box Plot for this data. When we include the check box for labeling outliers, the box plot gives an overall visualization of the data.

Interpreting a boxplot can be done once you understand what the different parts mean on a box and whisker diagram. The line splitting the box in two represents the median value. This shows that 50% of the data lies on the left-hand side of the median value and 50% lies on the right-hand side. The left edge of the box represents the lower quartile; it shows the value at which the first 25% of the data falls up to. The right edge of the box shows the upper quartile; it shows that 25% of the data lies to the right of the upper quartile value. The single points on the diagram show the outliers.

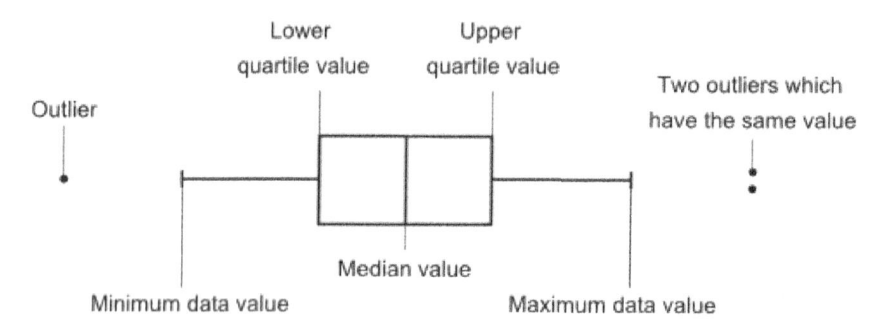

Box plots are very useful in interpreting the data since it gives a visualization of many important features present in the data. These features include;
- Showing the average (median) score of the data.
- Showing the skewness of the data; is the data distributed normally or skewed either to the right of left.
- Showing the dispersion (also called variability, scatter, or spread) of the data and the extent to which the data is bunched together or spread out.
- Sowing any outliers that may be present in the data.

Box plots can help us visualize how the data is spread out across the quartiles. Each section of the Box plot contains 25%, or one-quarter, of the data. We should select Boxplot elements and Label Outliers in the Boxplot settings.

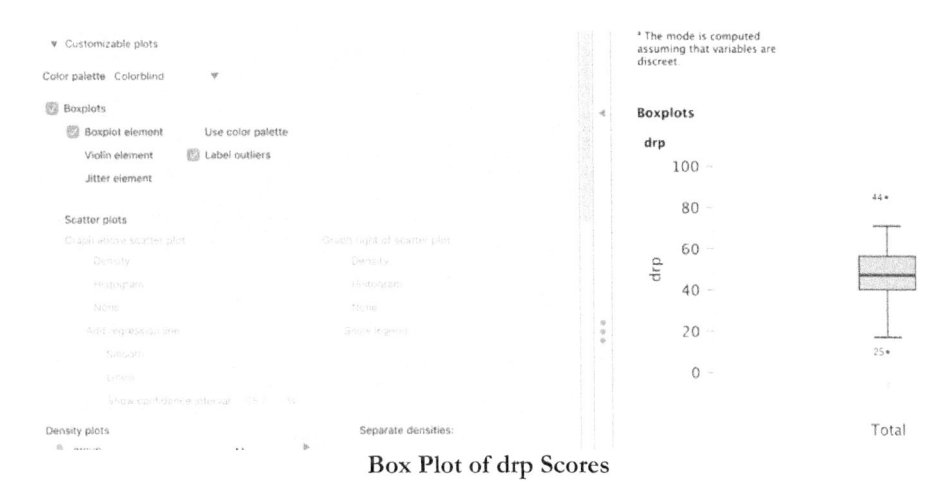

Box Plot of drp Scores

In the case of our Directed Reading Power assessment scores, we can notice from the Box plot that the lowest quartile of scores is more spread out than the upper quartile of scores. This could be something to consider as we begin analyzing the data. Outliers are labeled with the row number for that participant.

Continuous Data SPLIT by Categorical Data

Reviewing continuous data split by categorical grouping data can provide insights into possible comparisons between groups.

JASP has the capability to create graphs that are "Split" by some other variable in your data. For example, in this case we could examine the Directed Reading Program assessment and how they are represented within the treatment group, or the directed reading activities group, and the control group.

To create these split graphs, move the main variable into the Variable box and move the organizing variable into the "Split" box. We can use the same settings from the Statistics tab to compare the Measure of Central Tendency and the spread between two or more groups.

Quantitative Analysis

Results

Descriptive Statistics

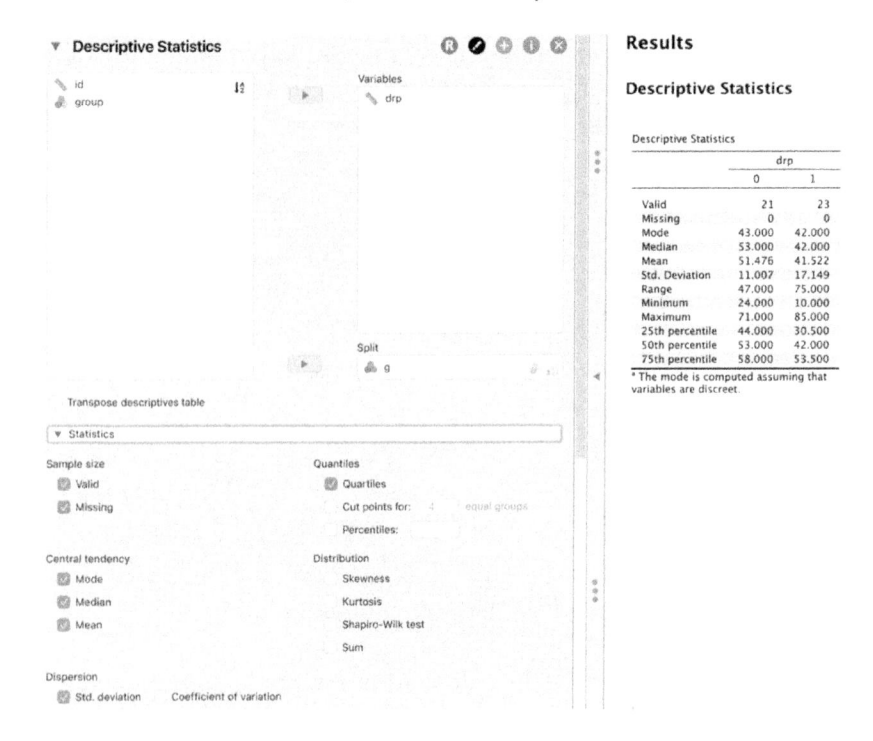

	drp 0	drp 1
Valid	21	23
Missing	0	0
Mode	43.000	42.000
Median	53.000	42.000
Mean	51.476	41.522
Std. Deviation	11.007	17.149
Range	47.000	75.000
Minimum	24.000	10.000
Maximum	71.000	85.000
25th percentile	44.000	30.500
50th percentile	53.000	42.000
75th percentile	58.000	53.500

*The mode is computed assuming that variables are discreet.

Be sure to also select **Basic Plots** to represent the data. Distribution plots as well as Dot Plots can show data features.

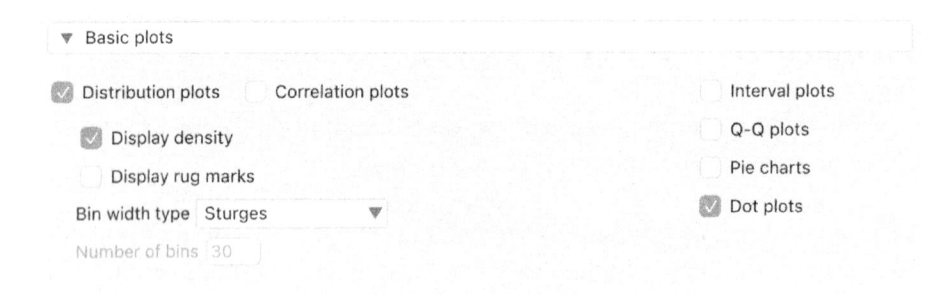

Plots Setting Window

In the case of Continuous data that has been split by some selected category, in this case we are considering the drp scores split across treatment/control groups, differences between the groups can be observed.

When exploring continuous data "split" by some categorical data, the Distribution plot with "Display density" checked may be a useful visualization to see if the data has a generally normal distribution.

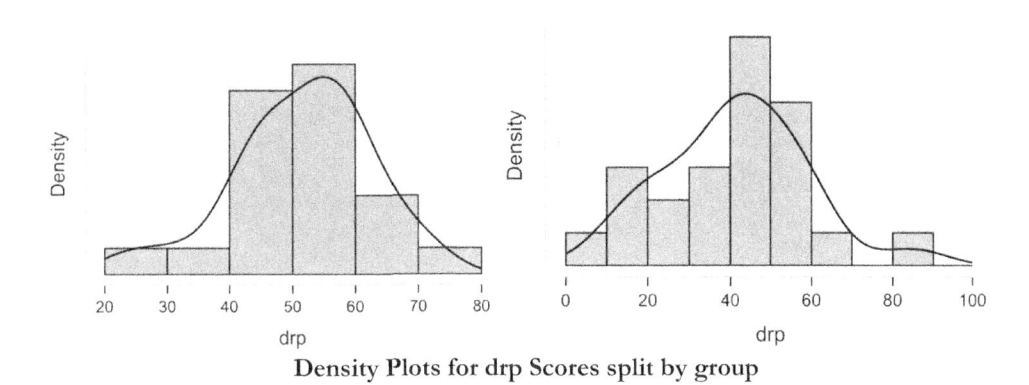

Directed Reading activities Group   Control Group

Density Plots for drp Scores split by group

By using the **Customized Plots** tab, exploring the descriptive statistics for our data through the box plot, questions may begin to emerge and suggest directions for further investigation. In the case of our drp scores we may notice that the median score for the directed reading activities group is higher than the control group's median score. We can also see that the drp assessment for control group seems to have a greater spread and variability.

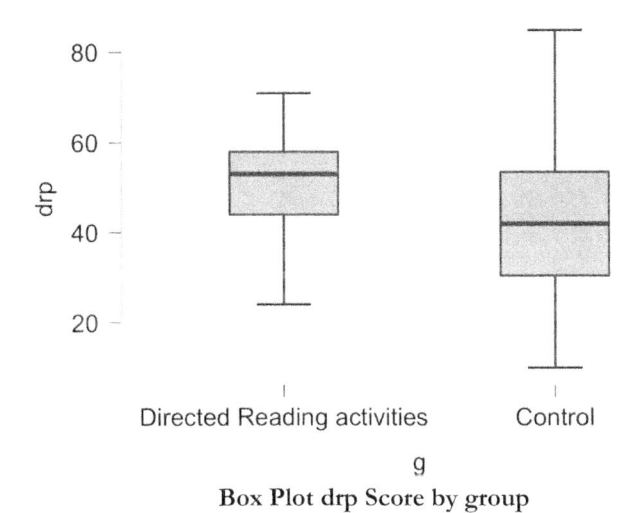

Box Plot drp Score by group

Once the data's descriptive statistics has been explored, patterns may have emerged, and questions may have arisen based on the data. We are now ready to begin inferential statistical analysis.

Quantitative Analysis

Section III: Frequentist Approaches

Chapter 6
Relationship Analysis with t-Test

When to use t-Tests – in plain English

The t-Test is used when you want to compare TWO means or averages, and it is used to ONLY compare two means. The means just need to be some number, or continuous variable. This number can be an assessment score, time, distance, or even a count. The important part of the t-Test is that you are analyzing two means. These two means could come from your study group and some known population mean, referred to as a One Sample t-Test. They could be two means from your study group just collected at different times or over time, referred to as a Paired Samples t-Test. The two means could also be the same mean taken from two groups within your study, referred to as an Independent Samples t-Test. It does not really matter where the two means come from, there just has to be only two. If you have this part done, then there is a t-Test for you to use.

When conducting inferential data analysis, there is a basic process that we follow for every method. This sequence of steps can serve as a guide when learning the analysis process.

Basic Quantitative Analysis Process (t-Test)

Check the Assumptions
- *The assumptions help us determine the most appropriate analysis method when deciding between parametric and nonparametric methods.*
- *If the assumptions are met, then use the parametric methods. If they are not met, use one of the nonparametric methods.*

Review for Statistical Significance
- *A p-value less than 0.05 is accepted as statistically significant in the Social Sciences.*
- *A p-value grater or equal to 0.05 is accepted as not statistically significant in the Social Sciences.*
- *If the result is statistically significant, go to the next steps. If a result is not statistically significant, the next steps are not necessary.*

Review the Effect Size
- *The effect size will provide information about the magnitude or how obvious the reported differences are in the real world and in the context of the data.*

Review the Confidence Interval
- *The confidence interval will help us understand the differences if we resampled the data from our population. It represents the range of values we are likely to find in the population.*

Report the Results
- *After the analysis, you will want to report the results. If the results were not significant, simply state that the results were "not statistically significant. Significant results are reported in a formal format.*

t-Test Analysis (Continuous Differences, two groups)

The t-Test compares two averages, or means, and indicates if they differ from one another. The t-Test also tells you the significance of those differences. In other words, the t-Test lets you know if those differences could have occurred by chance.

There are three t-Tests methods available in JASP;

1. **Independent Samples t-Test**: Compares the means scores of two groups on a given variable.
2. **Pair Samples t-Test**: Compares the means of two variables for one group. This is commonly used for groups with pre- and post- test measures.
3. **One Sample t-Test**: Compares the mean score of a sample to a known mean score. The known mean is typically referred to as the known or hypothesized population mean.

Independent Samples t-Test

The following examples will use the Directed Reading Activities dataset from the JASP Data Library. The question we are asking this data is whether or not there are differences in the Degree of Reading Power assessment scores between the group of students who received direct instruction in these reading skills and those who did not. We could also ask the question, "Is there a relationship between a student's Degree of Reading Power assessment and participation in directed reading activities?"

Open the Directed Reading Activity dataset from the JASP data Library
Data Library > Categories > t-Test > Directed Reading Activities

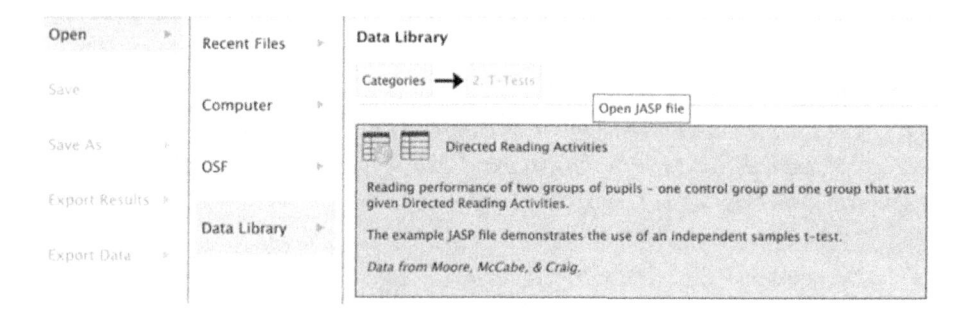

Using the t-Test tab, select "Independent Samples T-Test" from the pull-down menu. With Independent Samples we will investigate the differences between TWO groups on the SAME measure.

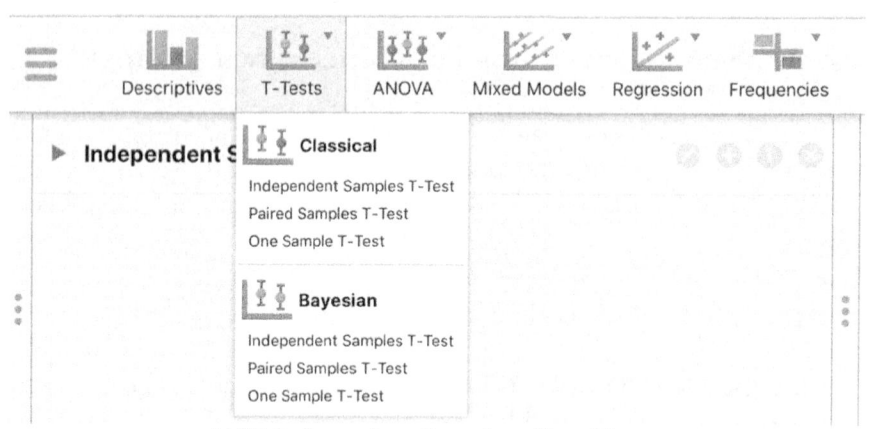

JASP Independent Samples t-Test Menu

When using the Independent Samples t-Test select the test variable for the dependent variable window and the groups or factor for the grouping variable window. Be sure that the grouping variable only contains two grouping factors.

The "g" variable has been labeled with "Directed Reading Activity" and "Control" groups for clarity when the results tables are produced.

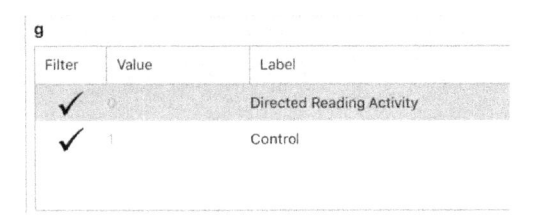

g		
Filter	Value	Label
✓	0	Directed Reading Activity
✓	1	Control

In this example we will be looking for differences in the Degree of Reading Power assessment scores between the group of students who received direct instruction in these reading skills and those who did not.

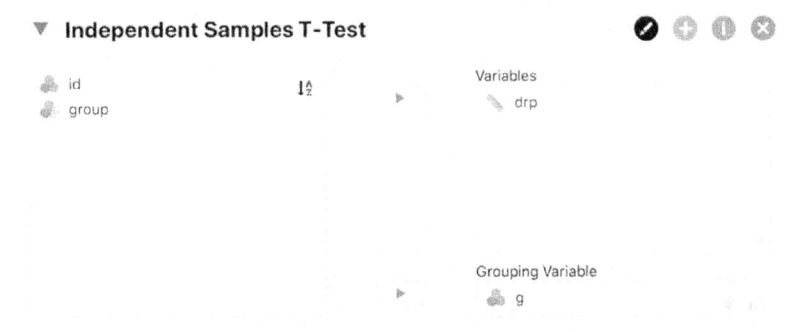

Independent t-Test Sample Window

If you select a grouping variable that contains more than two groups, the JASP results window will give an error message.

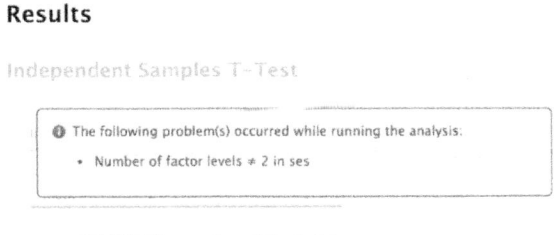

JASP Grouping Variable error message

We will also use the menu below the variable window to select the settings needed for this analysis. We will look more closely at each setting.

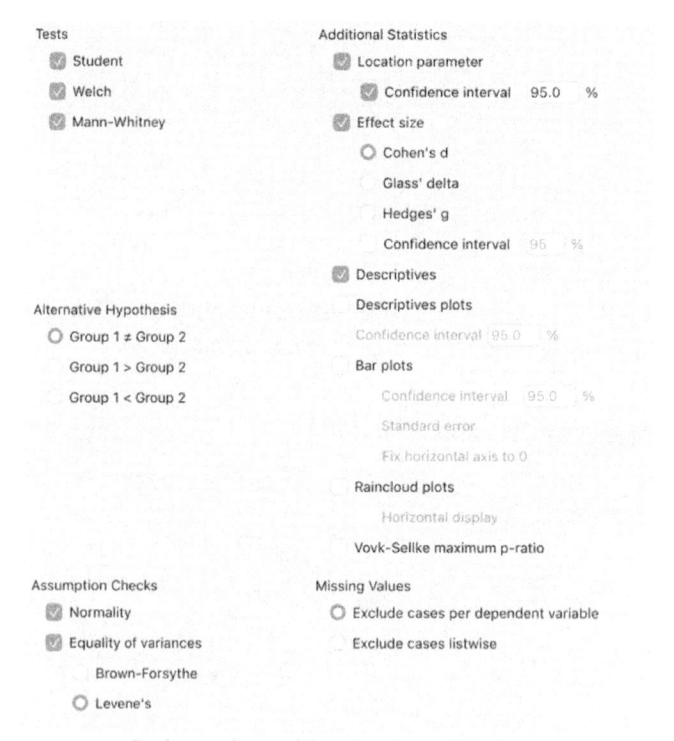

Independent t-Test Settings Window

The hypothesis that we will use in this example is that the Degree of Reading Power (drp) scores are different between the directed reading group and the control group. Our hypothesis does not indicate a direction for the differences or assume which group might outperform the other. This is indicated with the Alt. Hypothesis setting "Group 1 ≠ Group 2".

In the Tests setting, we can select the Student's t-Test, the Welch t-Test, or the Mann-Whitney test. Student's t-Test has two assumptions; 1) the data has a generally normal distribution and 2) the data does not exhibit significant variation. Student's t-Test is used to analyze parametric data. The assumption checks section of the settings allows us to verify these assumptions.

There are two nonparametric test available in JASP. Welch's test assumes normality but not equal variances. The Mann-Whitney test assumes equal variances but not normality.

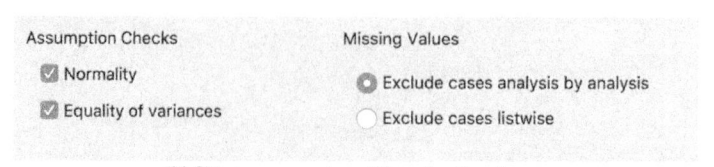

JASP Assumption Checks Settings

The Assumptions Check setting will analyze both the normality and equality of variance within the data. The results of this assumptions check will direct our analysis to either the Student's t-Test, Welch's t-Test, or Mann-Whitney. Recall that the mathematical assumption check for normality can be influenced by sample size, so a researcher should check the normality of the data both mathematically and graphically.

We will also check the settings to calculate the effect size (Cohen's d) and to produce a descriptives table for the assessment scores. In addition, we will select the 95% confidence interval to be displayed.

Interpreting the Results Tables for Independent Samples t-Test (Directed Reading)

The results tables below were produced using the Directed Reading Activity data found in the JASP Data Library. Theses tables represent the Independent Samples t-Test for differences in assessment scores between our two groups.

Check Assumption. Recall that the Student's t-Test assumes that your data generally has a normal distribution and that there is not significant variance within the data. The Welch and Mann-Whitney t-Tests do not require these assumptions to be met.

When reviewing the results of the assumption checks tables, a p-value is less than 0.05 indicates that the data varies significantly from normality and/or equal variance, thus we would use the appropriate t-Test. If the p-values are greater than 0.05 then we can assume that the assumptions have been met and our data meets the requirements of normality and equal variance, allowing us to use the Student's t-Test.

Test of Normality (Shapiro-Wilk)

		W	p
drp	Directed Reading Activity	0.966	0.652
	Control	0.972	0.732

Note. Significant results suggest a deviation from normality.

The Test of Normality (Shapiro-Wilk) show that the data we are analyzing meet the assumptions for normality, since the p-vales are greater than 0.05 suggesting that the data does not differ from normal, or parametric, data distributions.

Test of Equality of Variances (Levene's)

	F	df	p
drp	2.362	1	0.132

Quantitative Analysis

Levene's Test of Equality of Variances has a p-value greater than 0.05, indicating that our data has equal variance. In this example, the drp data meets both assumptions of normality and equal variance, therefore it is appropriate to use the Student's t-test for our analysis.

Review the p-Value. With these assumptions met, we can move on to the Student's t-Test. The Welch and Mann-Whitney results can be ignored, or you can uncheck those from the settings and the results table will update to only show the Student's t-Test results.

Independent Samples T-Test

	Test	Statistic	df	p	Location Parameter	SE Difference	95% CI for Location Parameter Lower	95% CI for Location Parameter Upper	Effect Size	SE Effect Size
drp	Student	2.267	42.000	0.029	9.954	4.392	1.091	18.818	0.684	0.320
	Welch	2.311	37.855	0.026	9.954	4.308	1.233	18.676	0.691	0.320
	Mann-Whitney	348.000		0.013	10.000		2.000	19.000	0.441	0.174

Independent Samples t-Test Results Table

The results of the Student's t-Test indicate that the differences in assessment scores are significantly different between the two groups (p = 0.029). We can "reject the null hypothesis" that there are not any differences and state that there is a relationship between the directed reading activities and the degree of reading power (drp) assessment.

Review the Effect Size. Cohen's d effect size estimate (d = 0.684) suggests that there is a medium effect size of the reading activities on the drp assessment score.

Review the Confidence Interval. The 95% Confidence Interval for this analysis suggest that in the general population of 3rd graders, we could expect to see a difference in their scores from 1.09 points to 18.8 points between the two groups.

The **descriptives** table allows for the examination of the actual differences between the two groups. Here we find that the Directed Reading Activity group had a mean assessment score of 51.48 points while the control group that did not participate in these activities had a mean assessment score of 41.52 points.

Group Descriptives

	Group	N	Mean	SD	SE
drp	Directed Reading Activity	21	51.48	11.01	2.40
	Control	23	41.52	17.15	3.57

Report the Results. In Social Science research, results are typically reported using the American Psychological Association (APA) format.

Basic Format
t(df) = t-value, "*p* < or =" p-value (d = Cohen's d value). Report details about the 95% CI.
- df is degrees of freedom from "df" column.
- t-value comes from "Statistic" column.
- p-value comes from "p" column. If an exact value is listed use "p = ___".
- d is effect size and comes from "effect size" column.

Example for this analysis
The differences in directed reading assessment scores (drp) based on the use of the Directed Reading Program is statistically significant, t(42) = 2.267, p = 0.029 (d = -0.684), as shown by the Student's t-test. Students receiving the DRP curriculum scored approximately 4.3 points higher than students in the control group, with a 95% confidence interval for the mean difference of approximately 1 to 18 points difference, 95% CI [1.09, 18.81].

Interpreting the Results Tables for Independent Samples t-Test: Nonparametric Example (Eye Movement)

The Eye Movement study measured a participant's ability to recall words after reading them. One group was instructed to stare at one-point, fixed eye gaze, while memorizing the words and the other group was instructed to scan the page, horizontal eye gaze, while reading the words.

The results tables below were produced using the Eye Movement data found in the JASP Data Library. Theses tables represent the Independent Samples t-Test for differences in word recall scores between our two groups.

Open the Eye Movement dataset from the JASP data Library
Data Library > Categories > t-Test > Eye Movement

Quantitative Analysis

Data Library

Categories → 2. T-Tests

Eye Movements

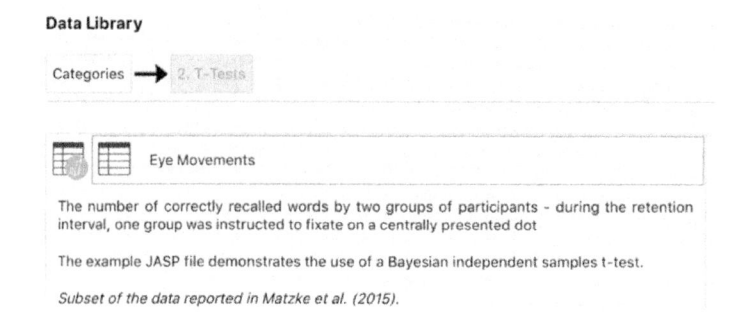

The number of correctly recalled words by two groups of participants - during the retention interval, one group was instructed to fixate on a centrally presented dot

The example JASP file demonstrates the use of a Bayesian independent samples t-test.

Subset of the data reported in Matzke et al. (2015).

The t-Test settings are the similar to our previous example.

[Screenshot of JASP t-Test settings panel showing ParticipantNumber variable, Dependent Variables: CriticalRecall, Grouping Variable: Condition. Tests: Student, Welch, Mann-Whitney. Alternative Hypothesis options: Group 1 ≠ Group 2, Group 1 > Group 2, Group 1 < Group 2. Assumption Checks: Normality, Equality of variances. Additional Statistics: Location parameter, Confidence interval 95.0%, Effect size (Cohen's d, Glass' delta, Hedges' g), Descriptives, Descriptives plots, Bar plots, Raincloud plots, Vovk-Sellke maximum p-ratio. Missing Values: Exclude cases per dependent variable, Exclude cases listwise.]

Check the Assumptions. Recall that the Student's t-Test assumes that your data generally has a normal distribution and that there is not significant variance within the data. Welch's test assumes normality but not equal variances. The Mann-Whitney test assumes equal variances but not normality.

When reviewing the results of the assumption checks tables, a p-value is less than 0.05 indicates that the data varies significantly from normality and/or equal variance, thus we would use the Welch or Mann-Whitney t-Test. If the p-values are greater than 0.05 then we can assume that the assumptions have been met and our data meets the requirements of normality and equal variance, allowing us to use the Student's t-Test.

The test for normality table shows that the data does not differ significantly from a normal distribution. The data we are analyzing meet the assumptions for normality, since the p-vales are greater than 0.05 suggesting that the data does not differ from normal, or parametric, data distributions.

Test of Normality (Shapiro-Wilk)

		W	p
CriticalRecall	Fixation	0.926	0.079
	Horizontal	0.959	0.396

Note. Significant results suggest a deviation from normality.

Levene's Test of Equality of Variances has a p-value less than 0.05 (p = 0.009), indicating that our data does not have equal variance. In this example, the Critical Recall of words data does not meet all assumptions of equal variance, therefore it is appropriate to use the Welch's t-Test for our analysis.

Test of Equality of Variances (Levene's)

	F	df	p
CriticalRecall	7.459	1	0.009

With these assumptions checked, we can move on to the Welch's t-Test.

Independent Samples T-Test

	Test	Statistic	df	p	Location Parameter	SE Difference	95% CI for Location Parameter Lower	95% CI for Location Parameter Upper	Effect Size	SE Effect Size
CriticalRecall	Student	2.845	47.000	0.007	4.412	1.551	1.292	7.531	0.813	0.309
	Welch	2.823	40.269	0.007	4.412	1.563	1.254	7.569	0.810	0.309
	Mann-Whitney	419.500		0.017	4.000		1.000	8.000	0.398	0.165

Independent Samples t-Test Results Table

Review the p-Value. The results of the Welch's t-Test indicate that the differences in recall scores are significantly different between the two group (p = 0.007). We can "reject the null hypothesis" that there are not any differences and state that there is a relationship between the number of recalled words and the participant's eye gaze.

Review Effect Size. Cohen's d (d = 0.810) suggests that there is a large effect size of eye gaze on the number of words that a participant can recall.

Review the 95% Confidence Interval. The confidence interval tells us that in the larger population, we could expect to find a difference between 1.2 and 7.5 words recalled based on the participant's eye gaze.

The **descriptives** table allows for the examination of the actual differences between the two groups. Here we find that the Fixed eye gaze group recalled an average of 15 words while the Horizontal eye gaze group recalled an average of about 11 words.

Group Descriptives

	Group	N	Mean	SD	SE
CriticalRecall	Fixation	24	15.292	6.376	1.301
	Horizontal	25	10.880	4.324	0.865

Report the Results. In Social Science research, results are typically reported using the American Psychological Association (APA) format.

Basic Format
t(df) = t-value, "$p <$ or $=$" p-value (d = Cohen's d value). Report details about the 95% CI.
- df is degrees of freedom from "df" column.
- t-value comes from "Statistic" column.
- p-value comes from "p" column. If an exact value is listed use "p = ___".
- d is effect size and comes from "effect size" column.

Example report for this analysis
The differences in the number of recalled words based on a participants fixed or horizontal eye gaze is statistically significant, t(40.3) = 2.82, p = 0.007 (d = 0.817), as shown by the Welch's t-test. Participant with a fixed eye gaze recalled approximately 5 more words than participants with a horizontal eye gaze, with a 95% confidence interval for the mean difference of approximately 1 to 8 words recalled, 95% CI [1.25, 7.56].

Paired Samples t-Test

The following examples will use the Moon and Aggression dataset from the JASP Data Library. The question we are asking this data is whether or not the participants have a different level of aggression or disruptions on full moon days versus other days. This is a Paired Sample t-Test since we are examining one group of participants with two measures: aggression on moon and non-moon days.

Open the Moon and Aggression dataset from the JASP data Library
    Data Library > Categories > t-Test > Moon and Aggression

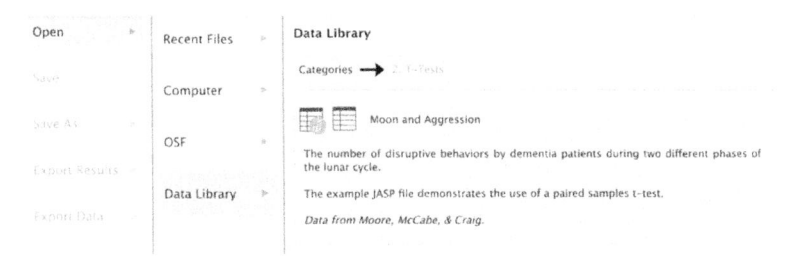

Using the t-Test tab, select Paired Samples t-Test. With Paired (Dependent) Samples we will investigate the differences between ONE group on the TWO different measures, such as two assessments or a pre-/post-assessment.

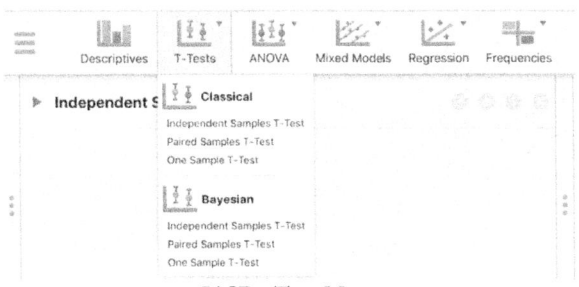

JASP t-Test Menu

When using the Paired Samples t-Test, in the dialogue box select the TWO variables. Use the arrow to move each variable into "Test Pair(s) window" or drag the desired variables into the window.

In this example we will be looking at the number of disruptions during a full moon and during other times that does not have a full moon.

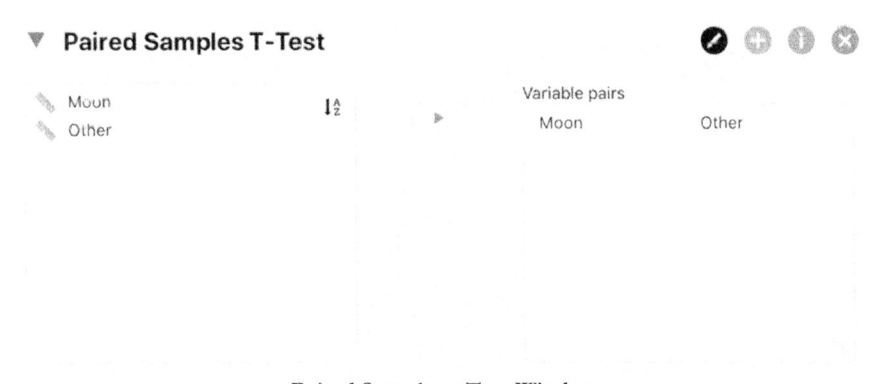

Paired Samples t-Test Window

Quantitative Analysis

We will also use the menu below the variable window to select the settings needed for this analysis. We will look more closely at each setting.

Paired Samples t-Test Settings Window

The hypothesis that we will use in this example is that the full moon number of disruptive behavior is different than the number of disruptive behaviors on other days without a full moon. Our hypothesis does not indicate a direction for the differences or assume which group might outperform the other. This is indicated with the Alt. Hypothesis setting "Measure 1 ≠ Measure 2".

In the Tests setting, we have selected both the Student's t-Test and the Wilcoxon signed-rank t-Test. Student's t-Test has two assumptions; 1) the data has a generally normal distribution and 2) the data does not exhibit significant variation. Student's t-Test is used to analyze parametric data. The assumption checks section of the settings allows us to verify these assumptions. The Wilcoxon signed-rank test does not make these assumptions, so it is used for non-parametric data.

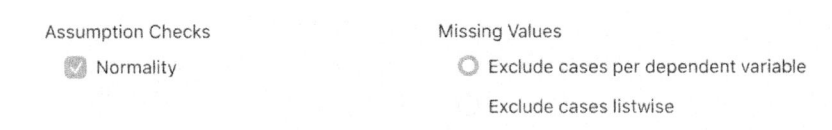

JASP Assumption Checks Settings

The Assumptions Check setting will analyze normality within the data. The results of this assumptions check will direct our analysis to either the Student's t-Test or Wilcoxon signed-rank t-Test. Recall that the mathematical assumption check for normality can be influenced by sample size, so a researcher should check the normality of the data both mathematically and graphically.

We will also check the settings to calculate the effect size (Cohen's d), confidence interval (under local parameters) and descriptives for the assessment scores.

Interpreting the Results Tables for Paired Samples t-Test (Moon & Aggression)

Check Assumption. Reviewing the Results window should begin with the Assumption Checks. Recall that the Student's t-Test assumes that your data generally has a normal distribution within the data. The Wilcoxon Signed-rank test does not require this assumption to be met.

When reviewing the results of the assumption checks tables, a p-value is less than 0.05 indicates that the data varies significantly from normality and/or equal variance, thus we would use the Wilcoxon signed-rank t-Test. If the p-values are greater than 0.05 then we can assume that the assumption has been met and our data meets the requirements of normality, allowing us to use the Student's t-Test.

Test of Normality (Shapiro-Wilk)

		W	p
Moon	Other	0.913	0.148

Note. Significant results suggest a deviation from normality.
Normality Check Table

The results indicate that the Test of Normality is not significant (p = 0.148), therefore we can assume that the data has a generally normal distribution, allowing for the use of the Student's t-Test.

Review the p-Value. The Paired Samples t-Test table indicates that the differences in aggression or disruptive behavior on full moon days compared to other days is statistically significant (p < 0.001). With this result we can reject the null hypothesis that there is not a difference and state that there is a relationship between disruptive behavior and days with a full moon.

Paired Samples T-Test

Measure 1	Measure 2	Test	Statistic z	df	p	Location Parameter	SE Difference	95% CI for Location Parameter Lower	95% CI for Location Parameter Upper	Effect Size	SE Effect Size
Moon	- Other	Student	6.45	14	< .001	2.43	0.38	1.62	3.24	1.67	0.49
		Wilcoxon	119.00 3.35		< .001	2.57		1.58	3.32	0.98	0.29

Paired Samples t-Test Results Table

Review the Effect Size. The data has a large effect size (d = 1.67). The large effect size suggests that the differences in aggression on full moon days and non-full moon days should be visible and obvious.

Review the 95% Confidence Interval. The confidence interval tells us that in the difference in "aggression" on full moon days compared to non-full moon days we could expect in the lager population is between 1.6 and 3.24 aggressive acts.

Descriptives

	N	Mean	SD	SE
Moon	15	3.02	1.50	0.387
Other	15	0.59	0.45	0.115

The descriptives table allows us to analyze the difference in means between the measures on full moon days and other days for these participants. Here we see that the participants had an average of 3 disruptive acts on full moon days compared to an average of 0.59 disruptive acts on other days.

Report the Results. In Social Science research, results are typically reported using the American Psychological Association (APA) format.

Basic Format
t(df) = t-value, "p < or =" p-value (d = Cohen's d value). Report details about the 95% CI.
- df is degrees of freedom from "df" column.
- t-value comes from "Statistic" column.
- p-value comes from "p" column. If an exact value is listed use "p = ___".
- d is effect size and comes from "effect size" column.

Example report for this analysis
The differences in the number of disruptions noted for participants based on a full moon present or not is statistically significant, t(14) = 6.52, p < 0.001 (d = 1.66), as shown by the Paired Samples t-test. Participant exhibited

approximately 2.43 more disruptions during a full moon than when there was not a full moon, with a 95% confidence interval for the mean difference of approximately 1.6 to 3 disruption, 95% CI [1.62, 3.24].

Nonparametric Paired Sample t-Test. When the assumptions check indicates that we should use the nonparametric method for the paired sample t-test, called the Wilcoxon test, follows the same procedures as other t-test methods.

One Sample t-Test

The following examples will use the Directed Reading Activity dataset from the JASP Data Library. The question we can ask this data is whether or not there are differences in the students' Directed Reading Power (drp) scores compared to a national average Directed Reading Power (drp) score?

Open the Directed Reading Activity dataset from the JASP data Library
    Data Library > Categories > t-Test > Directed Reading Activities

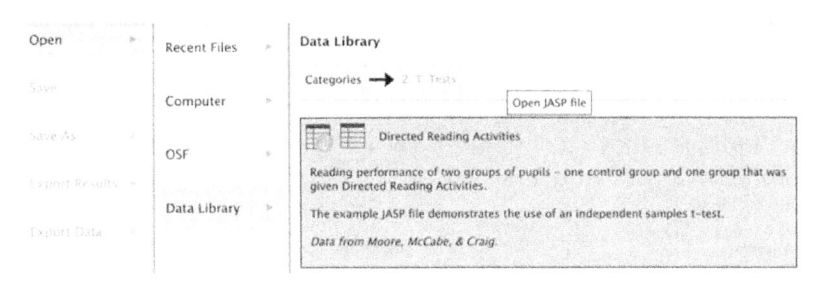

Using the t-Test tab, select One Sample t-Test. With One Sample t-Test we will investigate the differences between one group's performance on a measure compared to some known average on the SAME measure.

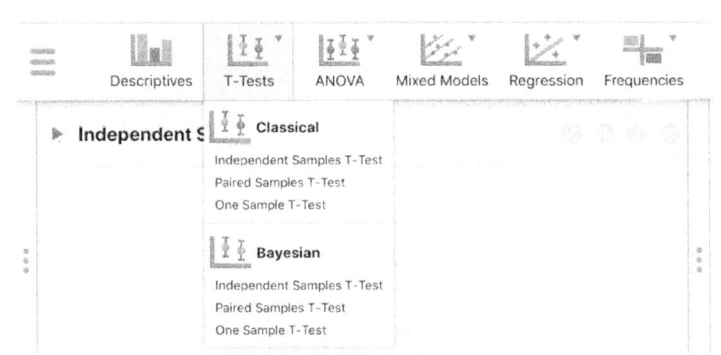

JASP One Sample t-Test Menu

When using the One Sample t-Test dialogue window, select the test variable. Be sure to move the measure to be compared into the test variable window.

Quantitative Analysis

Move the variable by either highlighting the variable and clicking on the arrow next to the variable window or by dragging the variable into the window.

In this example we are testing the drp score in our data compared to the "National average" score of 59 points for the average third grader.

This comparison is a hypothetical example.

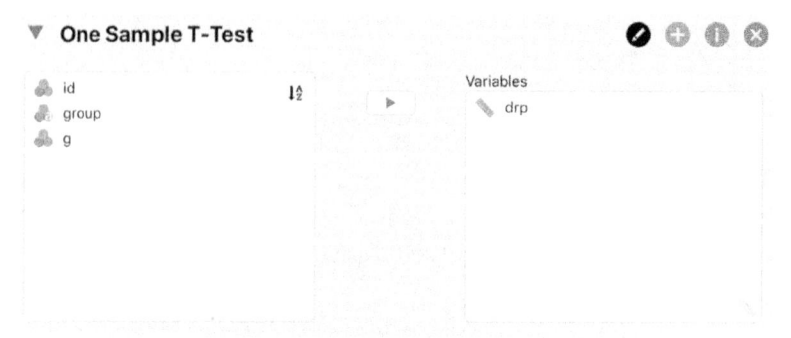

One Sample t-Test window

We will also enter the known average for this measure. The known average would come from a source outside of your own data collection, such as a norm referenced test or some national assessment measure that has a published average. In this example we are using a score of "59" to represent the known average for this assessment, as shown in the "Test Value" box.

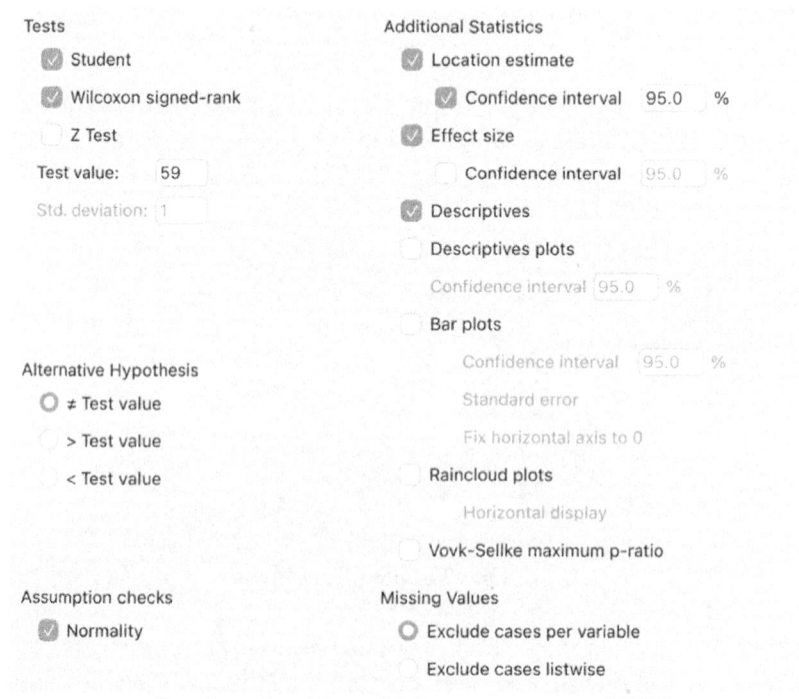

One Sample t-Test with known average of "59"

The hypothesis that we will use in this example is that the drp scores of our third-grade students is different than the drp national average. Our hypothesis does not indicate a direction for the differences or assume which group might outperform the other. This is indicated with the Alt. Hypothesis setting "≠ Test value".

In the Tests setting, we have selected both the Student's t-Test and the Wilcoxon signed-rank t-Test. Student's t-Test has two assumptions; 1) the data has a generally normal distribution and 2) the data does not exhibit significant variation. Student's t-Test is used to analyze parametric data. The assumption checks section of the settings allows us to verify these assumptions. The Wilcoxon signed-rank test does not make these assumptions, so it is used for non-parametric data.

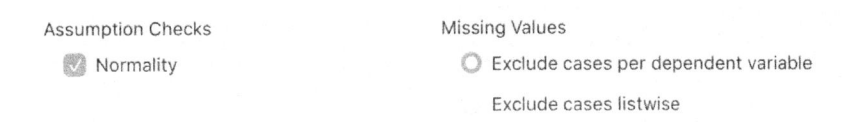

JASP Assumption Checks Settings

The Assumptions Check setting will analyze the normality within the data. The results of this assumptions check will direct our analysis to either the Student's t-Test or Wilcoxon signed-rank t-Test. Recall that the mathematical assumption check for normality can be influenced by sample size, so a researcher should check the normality of the data both mathematically and graphically.

We will also check the settings to calculate the effect size (Cohen's d) and to produce a descriptives table for the assessment scores.

Interpreting the Results Tables for One Sample t-Test (Directed Reading)

Check the Assumptions. We will begin with the assumption check for normality. Reviewing the Results window should begin with the Assumption Checks. Recall that the Student's t-Test assumes that your data generally has a normal distribution within the data. The Wilcoxon signed-rank t-Test does not require this assumption to be met.

When reviewing the results of the assumption checks tables, a p-value is less than 0.05 indicates that the data varies significantly from normality and/or equal variance, thus we would use the Wilcoxon signed-rank t-Test. If the p-values are greater than 0.05 then we can assume that the assumption has been met and our data meets the requirements of normality, allowing us to use the Student's t-Test.

Quantitative Analysis

Test of Normality (Shapiro-Wilk)

	W	p
drp	0.98	0.46

Assumption Checks Table

The results indicate that there is not a statically significant deviation from the normal distribution within our data (p = 0.46). Therefore, we can state that the data exhibits normality and the Student's t-Test is appropriate to use.

One Sample T-Test

Test		Statistic	df	p	Location Difference	95% CI Lower	95% CI Upper	Effect Size	SE Effect Size
drp	Student	-5.541	43	<.001	-12.727	-17.3	-8.0	-0.835	0.175
	Wilcoxon	90.500		<.001	-12.000	-17.000	-8.000	-0.809	0.173

Check the p-Value. The resulting output table will show the significance level (p-value), along with the effect size. In this case we find that the p-value for our measure when compared to the known mean is statistically significant (p < 0.001). Therefore, we can "reject the null hypothesis".

Check the Effect Size. In this analysis, the effect size can be considered a large effect size (d = -0.835). The sign of the effect size, either positive or negative, does not impact how we interpret the value. The sign just indicates which measure was larger; the sample mean or the test value mean.

Check the Confidence Interval. The confidence interval tells us that in the difference in drp test scores for our sample 3rd graders compared to the known average is between -8 points and -17.3 points. The negative sign of the confidence interval indicates that our sample test score mean is lower than the known average test value.

Descriptives

	N	Mean	SD	SE
drp	44	46.27	15.24	2.30

The descriptives table tells us that the drp mean score of 46 for the third graders in the sample data is not significantly different than the drp score mean of 59 for the larger third grader population.

Report the Results. In Social Science research, results are typically reported using the American Psychological Association (APA) format.

Basic Format
t(df) = t-value, "$p <$ or $=$" p-value (d = Cohen's d value). Report details about the 95% CI.
- df is degrees of freedom from "df" column.
- t-value comes from "Statistic" column.
- p-value comes from "p" column. If an exact value is listed use "p = ___".
- d is effect size and comes from "effect size" column.

Example report for this analysis
The differences in directed reading assessment scores (drp) when compared to the national average score of 59 points is statistically significant, t(43) = -5.54, p < 0.001 (d = -0.835), as shown by the Student's t-test. Students in this sample scored approximately 12 points lower than the national average, with a 95% confidence interval for the mean difference of approximately -8 to -17 points difference, 95% CI [-8.0, -17.3].

Nonparametric Paired Sample t-Test. When the assumptions check indicates that we should use the nonparametric method for the paired sample t-test, called the Wilcoxon test, follows the same procedures as other t-test methods.

Chapter 7
Relationship Analysis with ANOVA

When to use ANOVA – in plain English

I tend to think of the ANOVA test simply as a t-Test on steroids. With an ANOVA analysis, we are comparing three or more means from our study population. The means just need to be some number, or continuous variable. This number can be an assessment score, time, distance, or even a count. The important part of the ANOVA is that you are analyzing means. We do state above that the ANOVA is for three or more means, but you could perform an ANOVA test with just two means, but that would really just be wasting the power found in the ANOVA calculations. Afterall, if there are only two means then a t-Test would work just as well. With the dependent variable, the means that we are comparing, we would look for some groupings within our sample, such as occupation, ethnicity, race, etc. that has more than three groups.

Analysis of Variance (ANOVA)

The Analysis of Variance (ANOVA) is used to find differences between categorical variables with multiple groups (the independent factor) and a dependent variable such as a test score.

Basic Quantitative Analysis Process (ANOVA)

Check the Assumptions
- *The assumptions help us determine the most appropriate analysis method when deciding between parametric and nonparametric methods.*
- *If the assumptions are met, then use the parametric methods. If they are not met, use one of the nonparametric methods.*

Review for Statistical Significance
- *A p-value less than 0.05 is accepted as statistically significant in the Social Sciences.*
- *A p-value grater or equal to 0.05 is accepted as not statistically significant in the Social Sciences.*
- *If the result is statistically significant, go to the next steps. If a result is not statistically significant, the next steps are not necessary.*

Review the Effect Size
- *The effect size will provide information about the magnitude or how obvious the reported differences are in the real world and in the context of the data.*

Review Post Hoc Table
- *The post hoc analysis will show which groups are different from the others.*

Review the Confidence Interval
- *The confidence interval will help us understand the differences if we resampled the data from our population. It represents the range of values we are likely to find in the population.*

Report the Results
- *After the analysis, you will want to report the results. If the results were not significant, simply state that the results were "not statistically significant. Significant results are reported in a formal format.*

Using Univariate Analysis for One-Way ANOVA (Parametric Example)

The One-Way ANOVA will compare the means of multiple groups (3 or more) with a single dependent variable. This analysis will uncover differences between the groups. The example in this section will use the Pain Threshold data from the JASP Data Library.

The question we are asking this data is whether there is a relationship between hair color and pain threshold tolerances?

Open the Pain Thresholds dataset from the JASP data Library
Data Library > Categories > ANOVA > Pain Thresholds

Quantitative Analysis

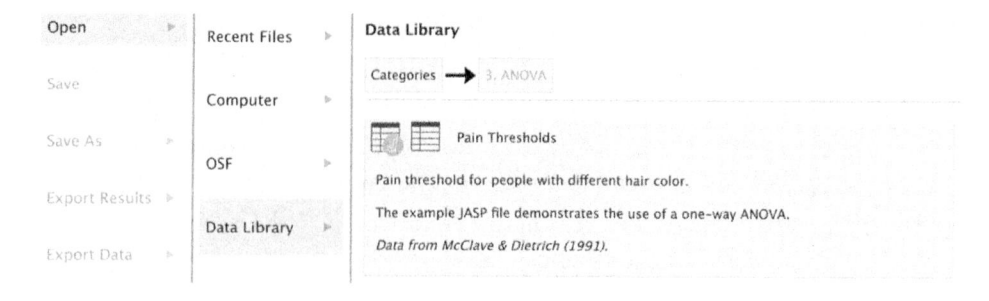

In JASP use the ANOVA tab to select the ANOVA function. In the ANOVA dialogue window, we will be entering the Dependent Variable as well as the Fixed Factor. By entering ONE fixed factor into this window, we will be performing a One-Way ANOVA.

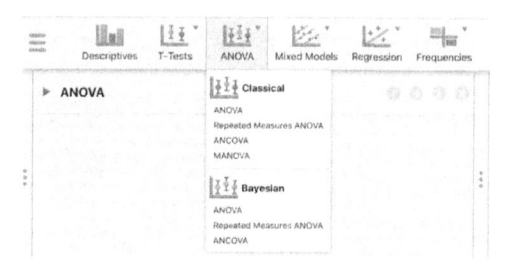

One Way ANOVA Menu

From the dialog box we will select the dependent and independent variables, here called fixed factors. The dependent variable, in the case of our sample data set, will be continuous data, such as a test score. In this example we will examine the pain tolerance scores.

One Way ANOVA Dialogue Window

Then select the independent variable to move into the Fixed Factors window. This will be a categorical variable that contains more than two groups. In this example we have selected "Hair Color".

We will also want to select the Descriptive statistics and the Effect size, eta squared (η^2) or partial eta squared (η^2_p), for this analysis.

Next we will be looking at the main settings to select from the pull-down menus to perform the One-Way ANOVA analysis. This guide will not describe each of the pull-down menu settings. We will focus on the main settings that are useful for the novice researcher to learn this method.

- ▶ Model
- ▶ Assumption Checks
- ▶ Contrasts
- ▶ Post Hoc Tests
- ▶ Descriptives Plots
- ▶ Marginal Means
- ▶ Simple Main Effects
- ▶ Nonparametrics

ANOVA Pull-Down Settings

The **Model settings** should show that "Hair Color" has been loaded into the Model Terms window. The other setting for "Sum of Squares" should remain at the default settings unless there is some rationale to change the Sum of Squares settings. The default setting for this function is "Type III".

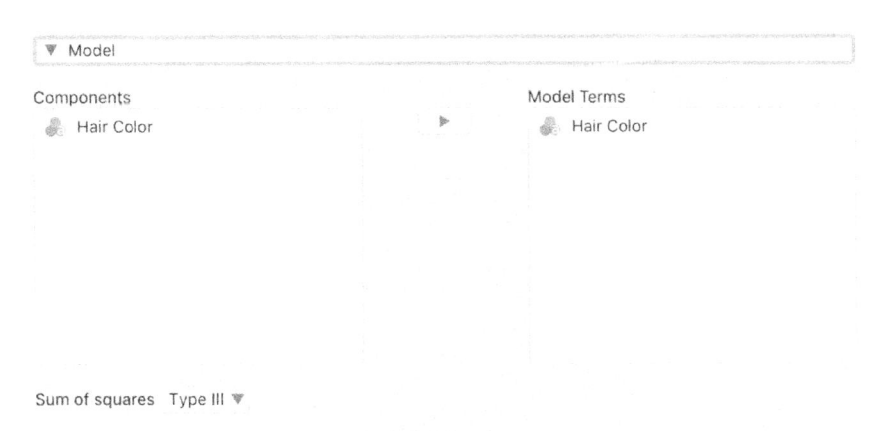

Model Setting

The **Assumption Checks** setting will show if the data exhibits an "equality of variance" in the distribution, as measured by the Levene's Statistic.

Homogeneity in the variance is one of the assumptions required to perform a standard ANOVA. The Q-Q plot of residuals, a graph of the residuals versus the expected order of the standard normal distribution, is often used as an assumption check as well. The Q-Q plot graph may be difficult for the novice researcher to interpret.

Assumption Checks Setting

The **Post Hoc Test** is a method to systematically test all the factors with one another to uncover differences between them. For the analysis type, we will select Standard, used for parametric data that meet the assumptions check.

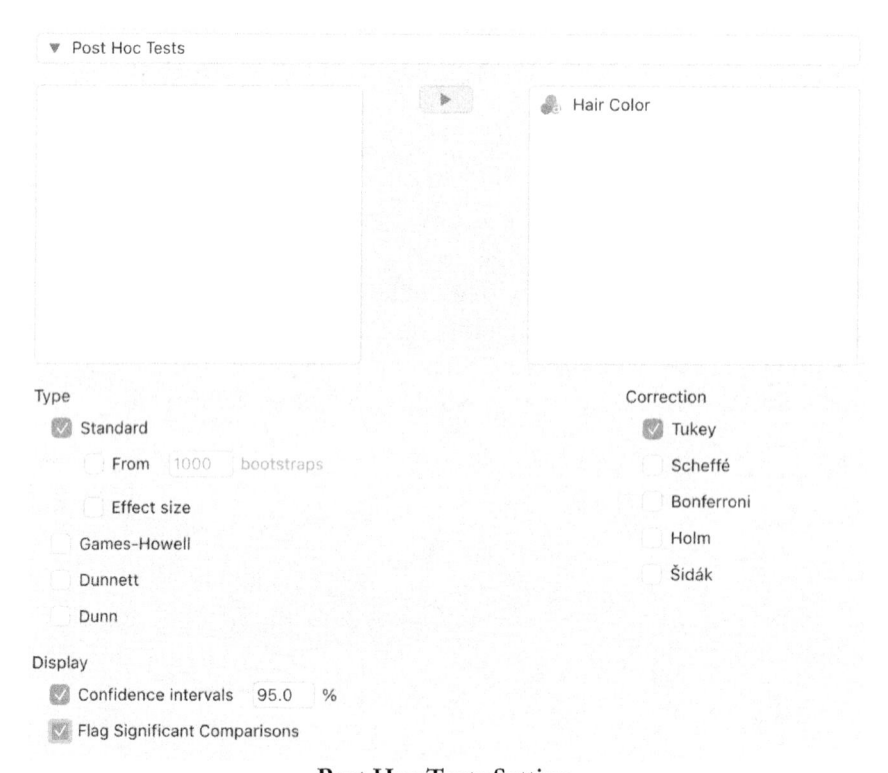

Post Hoc Tests Setting

A common Post Hoc correction method is Tukey, however, any of the Post Hoc analysis methods are appropriate to use. When beginning to learn about research analysis, the JASP presets should be sufficient.

In the post hoc setting tab we can also checked the confidence interval setting to display the 95% confidence interval for each pairwise comparison. Once all the settings have been selected you are ready to review the output tables created for the ANOVA analysis.

Interpreting Results Tables: One-Way ANOVA (Pain Threshold)

Once you run the One-Way ANOVA, the results will be in the Results Window of JASP. We will look at each table generated by the selected settings.

Check Assumptions. As with other analysis methods, reviewing the results window should begin with the Assumptions Check. Recall that the standard ANOVA assumes that your data generally has a normal distribution.

Assumption Checks
Test for Equality of Variances (Levene's)

F	df1	df2	p
0.49	3.00	15.00	0.69

When reviewing the results of the assumption checks tables, a p-value is less than 0.05 indicates that the data varies significantly from normality and/or equal variance, thus we would use the Kruskal-Wallis test. If the p-values are greater than 0.05 then we can assume that the assumptions have been met and our data meets the requirement of normality, allowing us to use the standard ANOVA.

In this example the assumption check p-value is greater than 0.05 (p=0.69), therefore the assumptions have been met and we can use the standard ANOVA results.

Review the p-Value. The first table generated by JASP is the overall standard ANOVA Results. The column of most interest here is the "p" column showing the p-value. We find that the p value is 0.004, making the differences in pain thresholds based on hair color statistically significant.

ANOVA - Pain Tolerance

Cases	Sum of Squares	df	Mean Square	F	p	η^2	η^2_p
Hair Color	1360.726	3	453.575	6.791	0.004	0.576	0.576
Residuals	1001.800	15	66.787				

Note. Type III Sum of Squares
ANOVA Output Table

Review the Effect Size. The column for effect size is labeled eta squared "η^2". In this data the overall effect size is large for at least one pairwise

Quantitative Analysis

comparison ($\eta^2 = 0.576$) indicating that any differences should be noticeable. We can also see that the eta squared effect size and the partial eta squared (η^2_p) effect size calculation for this data is the same.

Review the Post Hoc Results. The Post Hoc tables provide information about the various fixed factor pairings that resulted in the significant differences within the data.

Standard
Post Hoc Comparisons - Hair Color

		Mean Difference	95% CI for Mean Difference Lower	Upper	SE	t	p_{tukey}
Dark Blond	Dark Brunette	13.800	-1.097	28.697	5.169	2.670	0.074
	Light Blond	-8.000	-22.897	6.897	5.169	-1.548	0.436
	Light Brunette	8.700	-7.100	24.500	5.482	1.587	0.415
Dark Brunette	Light Blond	-21.800	-36.697	-6.903	5.169	-4.218	0.004**
	Light Brunette	-5.100	-20.900	10.700	5.482	-0.930	0.789
Light Blond	Light Brunette	16.700	0.900	32.500	5.482	3.046	0.037*

Note. P-value and confidence intervals adjusted for comparing a family of 4 estimates (confidence intervals corrected using the tukey method).
* $p < .05$, ** $p < .01$

Post Hoc Results Table

The Post Hoc Comparisons results table shows the differences among the groups more clearly. Here we can see that the difference in pain thresholds between the Dark Brunette group and the Light Blond group is statistically significant (p = 0.004). The results also show that the differences in pain thresholds between the Light Blond group and the Light Burnette group appears to be statistically significant (p =0.049).

The mean difference column of the Post Hoc table also shows the mean difference of pain tolerance scores between the groups. Here we notice that the Dark Brunette group's mean pain tolerance score was 21.8 points lower than the mean pain tolerance score for the Light Blond group. Also the Light Blond group had a pain threshold 16.7 points higher than the Light Brunette group.

Review the Confidence Interval. The 95% confidence interval shows that in the general population, we expect to see a difference of 6.9 to 36.6 points on the pain threshold between the Light Blond group and the Dark brunette group.

The confidence interval also shows that in the general population we could expect to see a difference of 0.09 to 16.7 points on the pain threshold scale between the Light Blond and the Light Brunette groups. We should note that the lower value in the confidence interval is very close to zero (0), which might mean that there might be very little difference between these groups.

Report the Results. In Social Science research, results are typically reported using the American Psychological Association (APA) format.

Basic Format
F(df, residual df) = F-value, p = _____, with a _____ effect size (partial eta squared/eta squared). Report details about the 95% CI.
- df is the value in the first row of the df column.
- Residual df is the value in the second row of the df column.
- F-values is in the F column of the ANOVA table.
- p represents the p-value in the "p" column.
- Effect size can be found in the η^2 or η^2_p columns.

Example report for this analysis.
The differences in response to pain between participants with different color hair is statistically significant, F(3, 15) = 6.791, p = 0.004 with a large effect size (η^2 = 0.576), as shown by the One-Way ANOVA. The light blond participants showed higher pain thresholds than the dark brunette participants by approximately 22 points 95% CI [6.9, 36.6] and the light brunette participants by approximately 16 points 95% CI [0.9, 32.57].

Using Univariate Analysis for One-Way ANOVA (Non-Parametric Example Kruskal-Wallis)

The Krusal-Wallis ANOVA will compare the means of multiple groups, 3 or more, with a single dependent variable. This analysis will uncover differences between the groups. When the data is non-parametric, does not conform to a Normal distribution, we must use the Kruskal-Wallis test.

The example in this section will use the Facebook Friends data from the JASP Data Library. The question we are asking this data is whether there is a relationship between the number of Facebook Friends and perceived social attractiveness?

Open the Facebook Friends dataset from the JASP data Library
Data Library > Categories > ANOVA > Facebook Friends

Quantitative Analysis

In JASP use the ANOVA tab to select the ANOVA function. In the ANOVA dialogue window, we will be entering the Dependent Variable as well as the Fixed Factor. By entering one fixed factor into this window, we will be performing a One-Way ANOVA.

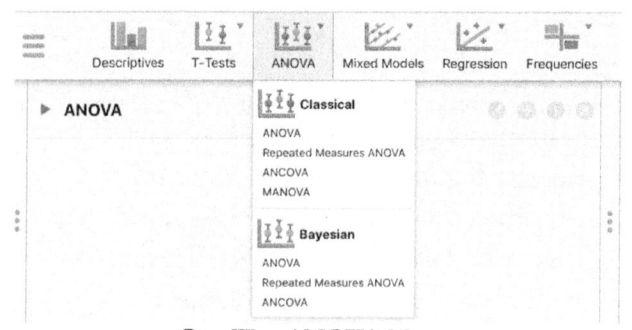

One Way ANOVA Menu

From the dialog box we will select the dependent and independent variables, here called fixed factors. The dependent variable, in the case of our sample data set, will be continuous data, specifically the "Score". In this example the score represents the social attractiveness score.

One Way ANOVA Dialogue Window

Then select the independent variable to move into the Fixed Factors window. This will be a categorical variable that contains more than two groups. In this example we have selected "Friends" as the fixed factor.

The other settings include the Descriptives as well as the effect size using the eta squared ($η^2$) and the partial eta squared ($η^2_p$).

Now we need to make sure that the Krskal-Wallis settings are displayed. At the bottom of the settings pull-down tab, we will need the "Nonparametrics" setting.

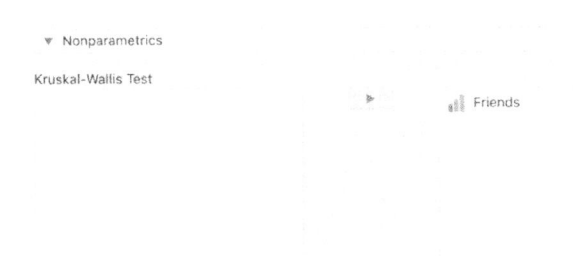

▼ Nonparametrics

Kruskal-Wallis Test

▶   Friends

Move the "Friends" factor from the left-window into the right-window. Moving the factor allows the Kruskal-Wallis results table to be displayed in the Results window.

Next we will be looking at the main settings to select from the pull-down menus to perform the One-Way ANOVA analysis.

▶ Model

▶ Assumption Checks

▶ Contrasts

▶ Post Hoc Tests

▶ Descriptives Plots

▶ Marginal Means

▶ Simple Main Effects

▶ Nonparametrics

ANOVA Pull-Down Settings

The **Model settings** should show that "Hair Color" has been loaded into the Model Terms window. The other setting for "Sum of Squares" should remain at the default settings unless there is some rationale to change the Sum of Squares settings. The default setting for this function is "Type III".

Quantitative Analysis

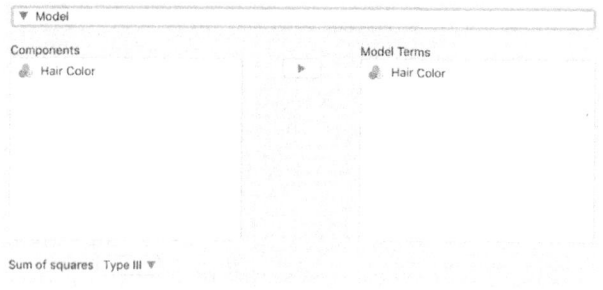

Model Setting

The **Assumption Checks** setting will show if the data exhibits an "equality of variance" in the distribution, as measured by the Levene's Statistic. Homogeneity in the variance is one of the assumptions required to perform a standard ANOVA. The Q-Q plot of residuals, a graph of the residuals versus the expected order of the standard normal distribution, is often used as an assumption check as well. The Q-Q plot graph may be difficult for the novice researcher to interpret.

Assumption Checks Setting

The **Post Hoc Test** is a method to systematically test all the factors with one another to uncover differences between them. A common Post Hoc correction method for the Kruskal-Wallis analysis in Dunn, with the Holm correction.

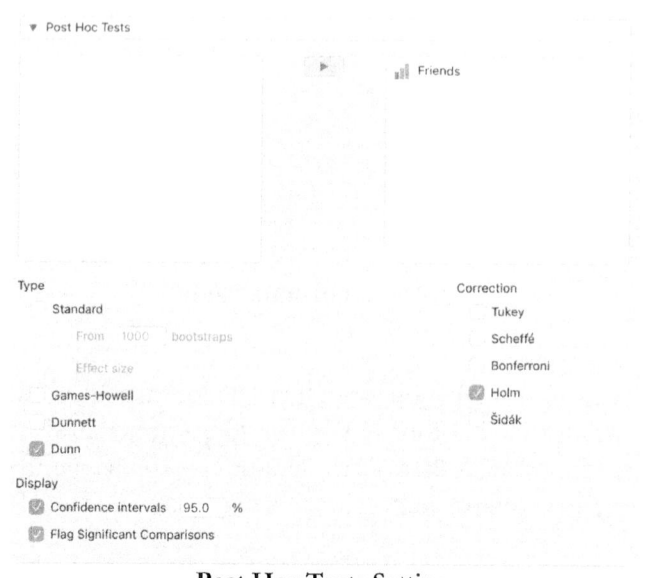

Post Hoc Tests Setting

Once all the settings have been selected you are ready to review the output tables created for the ANOVA analysis.

Interpreting Results Tables: One-Way ANOVA (Facebook Friends)

Once you run the One-Way ANOVA, the results will be in the Results Window of JASP. We will look at each table generated by the selected settings.

Review Assumptions. The first results table to examine is the Assumption Checks. As with other analysis methods, reviewing the results window should begin with the Assumption Checks. Recall that the standard ANOVA assumes that your data generally has a normal distribution. The Kruskal-Wallis test does not require this assumptions to be met.

Assumption Check
Test for Equality of Variances (Levene's)

F	df1	df2	p
2.607	4.000	129.000	0.039

When reviewing the results of the assumption checks tables, a p-value is less than 0.05 indicates that the data varies significantly from normality and/or equal variance, thus we would use the Kruskal-Wallis test. If the p-values are greater than 0.05 then we can assume that the assumptions have been met and our data meets the requirements of normality, allowing us to use the standard ANOVA.

In this example the assumption check p-value is less than 0.05 (p=0.039), therefore the assumptions have not been met and we must use the Kruskal-Wallis test results and the Dunn's Post Hoc table.

Review the p-Value. The Kruskal-Wallis table generated by JASP is the overall ANOVA results when the assumptions have not been met. The table that we will be concerned with is placed at the bottom of the output window, the Kruskal-Wallis test results table.

Kruskal-Wallis Test

Factor	Statistic	df	p
Friends	17.053	4	0.002

Kruskal-Wallis Output Table

By reviewing the Kruskal-Wallis output table, located at the end of the results window, we will be able to determine if there are statistically significant differences in this data. The results indicate that there is a statistically significant relationship between the social attractiveness scores and the number of friends (p = 0.002).

We can also review the descriptive statistics table to observe the differences between groups.

Descriptives - Score

Friends	N	Mean	SD	SE	Coefficient of variation
102	24	3.817	0.999	0.204	0.262
302	33	4.879	0.851	0.148	0.175
502	26	4.562	1.070	0.210	0.235
702	30	4.407	1.428	0.261	0.324
902	21	3.990	1.023	0.223	0.256

Review the Effect Size. The column we check for effect size is labeled eta squared or partial eta squared "η^2_p" column in the main ANOVA table. In this data the overall effect size is large for at least one pairwise comparison ($\eta^2_p = 0.114$) indicating that any differences should be noticeable.

ANOVA - Score

Cases	Sum of Squares	df	Mean Square	F	p	η^2	η^2_p
Friends	19.890	4	4.973	4.142	0.003	0.114	0.114
Residuals	154.867	129	1.201				

Note. Type III Sum of Squares

We should make note here that currently the effect size is not shown in the Kruskal-Wallis results table, but rather the Standard One-Way ANOVA results table. We can use this effect size measure since the calculation is based on the difference of means and standard deviation in the data. This will be the same regardless of which method is used for the analysis.

Review the Post Hoc. In this example, we will be using the Dunn post hoc table. ANOVA results often use a corrected p-value since these can become overestimated in the post hoc results. The Dunn's Post Hoc Comparison Table shows that the people with at least 302 friends exhibits significant differences compared to people with at least 102 friends (p < 0.001) and the group with at least 302 friends is significantly different (p = 0.021) than the group with at least 902 friends.

Dunn
Dunn's Post Hoc Comparisons - Friends

Comparison	z	W_i	W_j	p	p_{bonf}	p_{holm}
102 - 302	-3.720	46.250	84.909	< .001 ***	0.002 **	0.002 **
102 - 502	-2.373	46.250	72.269	0.018 *	0.177	0.141
102 - 702	-2.305	46.250	70.700	0.021 *	0.212	0.148
102 - 902	-0.665	46.250	53.952	0.506	1.000	1.000
302 - 502	1.244	84.909	72.269	0.213	1.000	0.643
302 - 702	1.454	84.909	70.700	0.146	1.000	0.643
302 - 902	2.863	84.909	53.952	0.004 **	0.042 *	0.038 *
502 - 702	0.151	72.269	70.700	0.880	1.000	1.000
502 - 902	1.612	72.269	53.952	0.107	1.000	0.642
702 - 902	1.519	70.700	53.952	0.129	1.000	0.643

* p < .05, ** p < .01, *** p < .001

Dunn's Post Hoc Results Table

Review the Confidence Interval. Unfortunately at this time the 95% Confidence Interval is not calculated in the Dunn Post Hoc table by JASP.

Report the Results. In Social Science research, results are typically reported using the American Psychological Association (APA) format.

Basic Format
H(df) = H-value, p = _____, with a _____ effect size (partial eta squared/eta squared). Report details about the 95% CI.
- df is the value in the Kruskal-Wallis table's the df column.
- H-values is in the Statistics column of the Kruskal-Wallis table.
- p represents the p-value in the "p" column.
- Effect size can be found in the η^2 or η^2_p columns of the ANOVA table.

Example report for this analysis.
The differences in preference ratings participants with number of Facebook friends is statistically significant, H(4) = 17.05, p = 0.002 with a large effect size (η^2 = 0.114), as shown by the Kruskal-Wallis ANOVA. The participants with 302 Facebook friends showed higher preference ratings than participants with 102 friends by approximately 1 point and participants with 902 friends by approximately 0.9 points.

Chapter 8
Associations with Correlation

When to use Correlations – in plain English

A correlation is really just asking "Do these two measurements line up when they are put on a graph?" In this case we are not looking for the dots on our graph to make a perfect line. Rather, we are looking to see if a line could be drawn through the dots so that most of the points are pretty close to the line. If we can make a line, the next step would be to create an equation so that if we know the value of one variable then it can be used to predict the value for the other variable. But this is for the next chapter.

Basic Quantitative Analysis Process (Correlation)

Check the Assumptions
- *The assumptions help us determine the most appropriate analysis method when deciding between parametric and nonparametric methods.*
- *If the assumptions are met, then use the parametric methods. If they are not met, use one of the nonparametric methods.*

Review for Statistical Significance
- *A p-value less than 0.05 is accepted as statistically significant in the Social Sciences.*
- *A p-value grater or equal to 0.05 is accepted as not statistically significant in the Social Sciences.*

- *If the result is statistically significant, go to the next steps. If a result is not statistically significant, the next steps are not necessary.*

Review the Correlation Coefficient
- *The correlation coefficient will provide information about the strength and direction of any association in the data.*

Report the Results
- *After the analysis, you will want to report the results. If the results were not significant, simply state that the results were "not statistically significant. Significant results are reported in a formal format.*

Correlations

The purpose of a correlation is to determine if there exists an association between two sets of data. The correlation does not take into account the various groups defined within the data, but merely tests if an association can be found.

In this Chapter we will explore various types of correlations;

- Using continuous data, both parametric and nonparametric. This type of correlation is performed by using either Pearson's r, Spearman's rho, or Kendal tau-b methods.
- Using ordinal ranked order data, such as Likert scale or rubric data. This type of correlation is referred to as a Spearman Ranked Order correlation.

When examining the r-coefficient, here labeled "Pearson's r", recall that correlation values range from -1 to 1, with a value of zero meaning no correlation exists. A value of -1 indicates perfect negative correlation while a value of 1 indicates perfect positive correlation. Negative correlation means that as one variable increases the other variable will decrease. Positive correlation means that as one variable increases the other variable also increases.

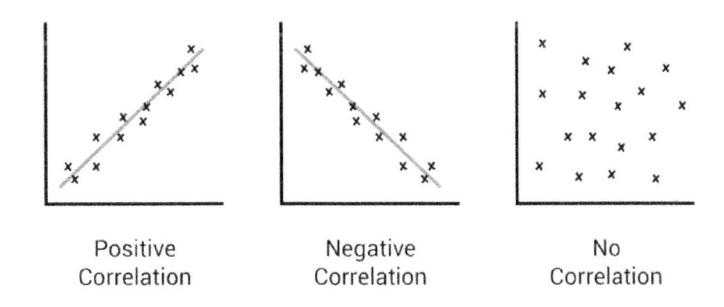

Positive Correlation | Negative Correlation | No Correlation

We must be careful when making statements about associations between data sets. Some of the observed correlations can be from chance while some of the correlation is due to the actual association between the data. We often remind ourselves that correlation does not equal causation.

r-value	Strength of Relationship
-1.0 to -0.8 or 0.8 to 1.0	Very Strong
-0.79 to -0.6 or 0.6 to 0.79	Strong
-0.59 to -0.4 or 0.4 to 0.59	Moderate
-0.39 to -0.2 or 0.2 to 0.39	Weak
-0.19 to 0.19	None or very weak

Correlation Strength of Relationship

The r-value, as described earlier, in the correlation table can indicate the strength of the association between the variables. The closer the r-value is to 1 or -1 the stronger the association. The r-value table provides a general rule of thumb for judging the strength of the association.

Correlation Analysis Parametric Data (Parametric Example)

In the following examples we will be using the Auction data from the JASP Data Library. We will be asking the data if there is a correlation between the age of an item being sold at auction, in this case they are antique clocks, and the final selling price.

Open the Auction dataset from the JASP data Library
Data Library > Categories > Regression > Auction

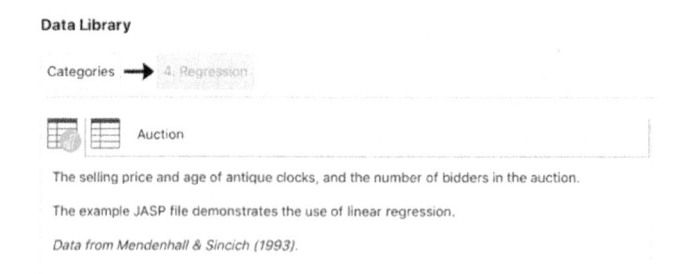

Use the Regression Tab, select Correlation Matrix. This will allow you to compare two sets of continuous data for an association . The Correlation Matrix test will perform a Pearson's Correlation on the data. Pearson's correlation is used for parametric data, as we have in this sample.

A JASP Guide: Foundational Methods

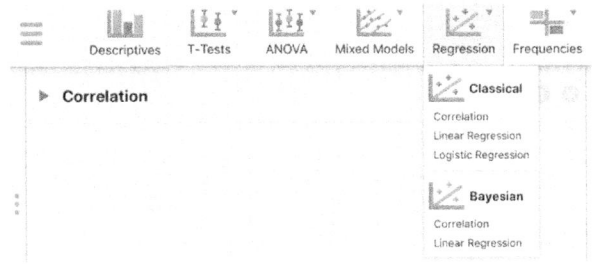

Bivariate Correlation Menu

From the dialog box move the variables into the Variables window. In this example we are using the age and price variables.

Correlation Matrix Dialogue Window

The other settings we will select are the Pearson Correlation Coefficient (normal/parametric data) and Reporting the significance. Our hypothesis is that the age of the clocks and the selling price are correlated.

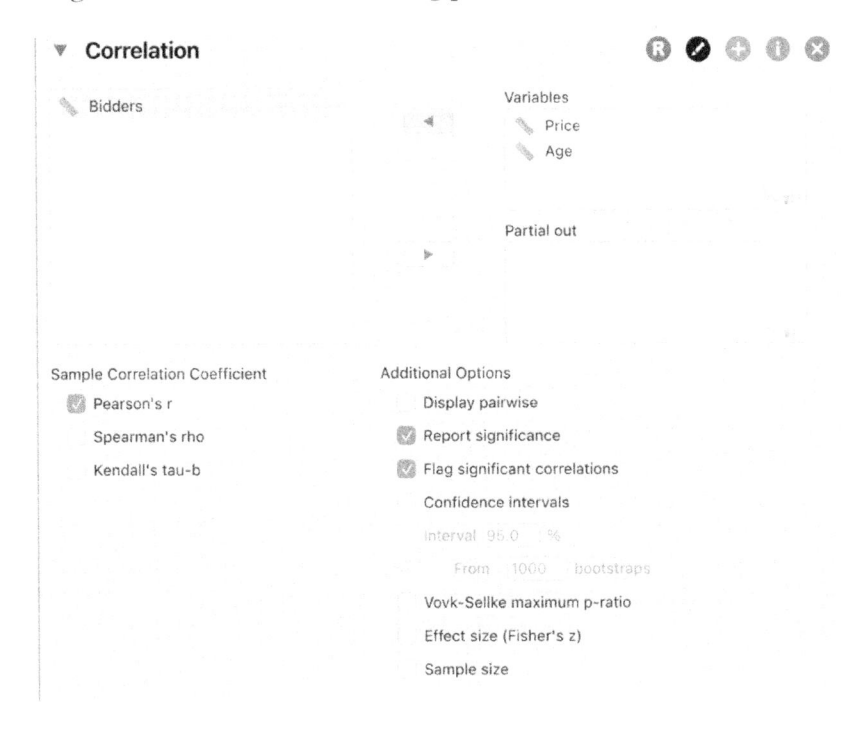

Quantitative Analysis

The data must also meet our assumptions check.

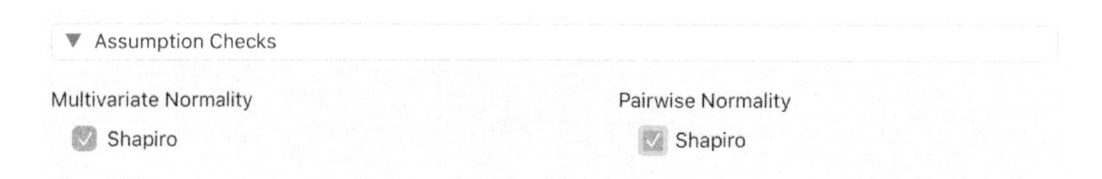

▼ Assumption Checks

Multivariate Normality
☑ Shapiro

Pairwise Normality
☑ Shapiro

The Shapiro test of normality will help determine the appropriate correlation coefficient to use in this analysis.

Interpreting Results Tables: Correlation Matrix (Auction)

Check Assumptions The first results table to examine is the Assumption Checks. As with other analysis methods, reviewing the results window should begin with the Assumption Checks. Pearson's r assumes that your data generally has a normal distribution. Spearman's rho does not require this assumption to be met.

When reviewing the results of the assumption checks tables, a p-value is less than 0.05 indicates that the data varies significantly from normality and/or equal variance, thus we would use the Spearman's rho. If the p-values are greater than 0.05 then we can assume that the assumptions have been met and our data meets the requirements of normality, allowing us to use Pearson's r.

Assumption checks

Shapiro-Wilk Test for Multivariate Normality

Shapiro-Wilk	p
0.943	0.093

Shapiro-Wilk Test for Bivariate Normality

			Shapiro-Wilk	p
Age	-	Price	0.943	0.093

The assumptions for this data is met, as shown by the assumption checks p-values being greater than 0.05 (p = 0.093). The Pearson's r correlation coefficient is appropriate to use in this case.

Review the p-Value. The second value in each row, labeled "p-value", will give the significance, or p-value, of the correlation Any correlation greater than +/-0.199 will be statistically significant. Here the correlation is statistically significant (p = < 0.001).

Pearson's Correlations

Variable		Price	Age
1. Price	n	—	
	Pearson's r	—	
	p-value	—	
2. Age	n	32	—
	Pearson's r	0.730***	—
	p-value	< .001	—

* p < .05, ** p < .01, *** p < .001

Pearson Correlation Table

Review the Correlation Coefficient. In correlations, the r-coefficient is the effect size. It carries more information about the association than the p-value.

The Pearson correlation value indicates the direction and strength of the association. In the example above we could state that the variables have a strong positive correlation, r = 0.730 (p < 0.01).

Report the Results. In Social Science research, results are typically reported using the American Psychological Association (APA) format.

Basic Format
r (N - 2) = Pearson's r-value, p < 0.001
- N-2 is the sample size, found in the "n" row of the table minus 2.
- Person's r-vale is located in the "Person's r" row of the table.
- p represents the p-value in the "p" row.

Example report for this analysis.
There is a strong positive correlation (r = 0.730) between the age of an antique clock and the selling price of that clock at auction.

Correlation Analysis Nonparametric Data (Nonparametric Example)

In the following examples we will be using the Exam Anxiety data from the JASP Data Library. We will be asking the data if there is a correlation between the time spent studying and a student's exam grade.

Open the Exam Anxiety dataset from the JASP data Library
Data Library > Categories > Regression > Exam Anxiety

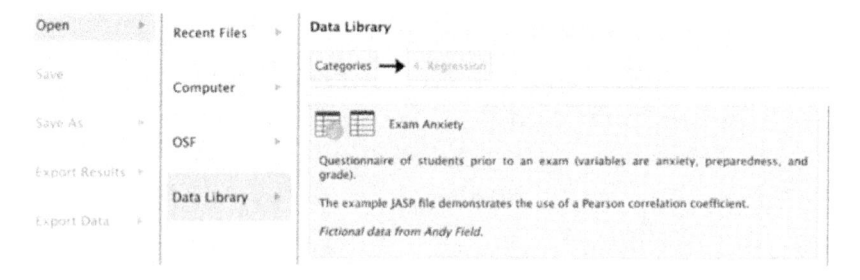

Use the Regression Tab, select Correlation Matrix. This will allow you to compare the data for an association. Spearman's Ranked correlation or the Kendall's tau-b is used for non-parametric data, as we have in this sample.

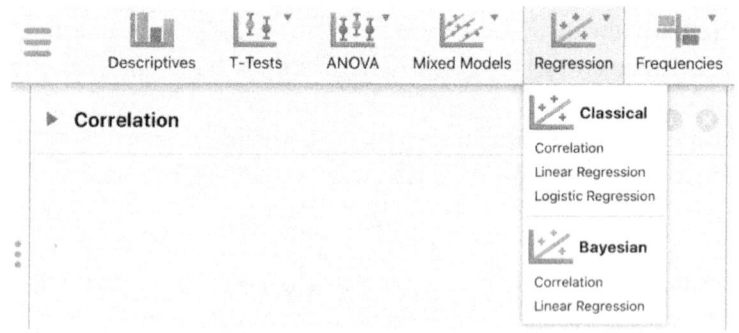

Bivariate Correlation Menu

From the dialog box move the variables into the variables window. In this example we are using the hours studying (Revise) and the exam grade (Exam).

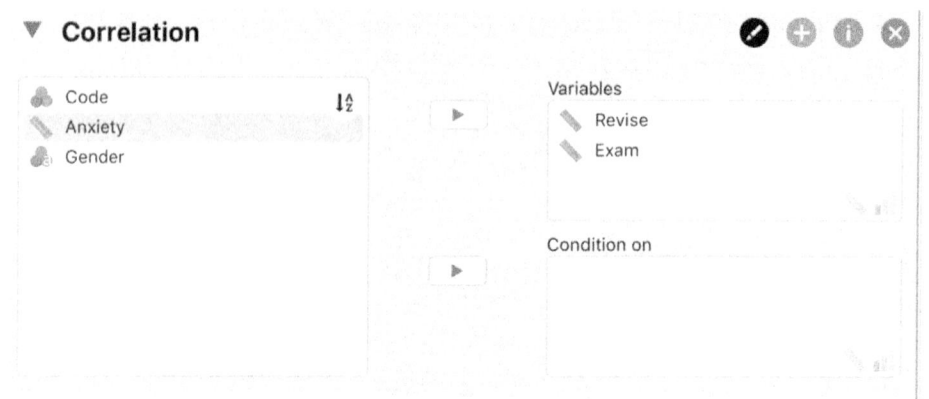

Correlation Matrix Dialogue Window

The other settings we will select are the Correlation Coefficient and Reporting the significance. Our hypothesis is that the time a student spends studying and the exam grade are correlated.

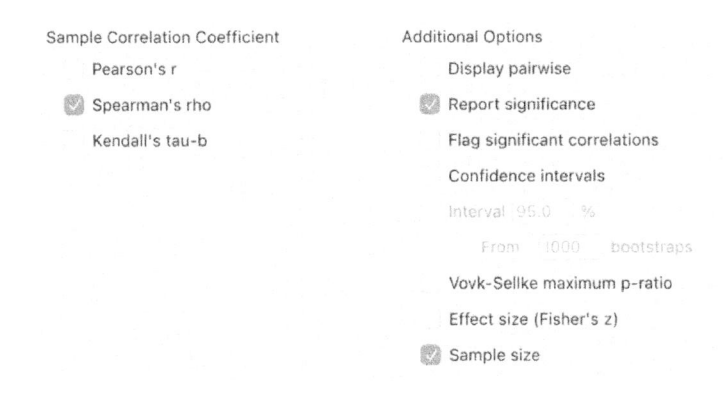

The data must also meet our assumptions check.

The Shapiro test of normality will help determine the appropriate correlation coefficient to use in this analysis; Pearson or Spearman.

Interpreting Results Tables: Correlation (Exam Anxiety)

Check the Assumptions. The first results table to examine is the Assumption Checks. As with other analysis methods, reviewing the results window should begin with the Assumption Checks. Pearson's r assumes that your data generally has a normal distribution. Spearman's rho does not require this assumption to be met.

When reviewing the results of the assumption checks tables, a p-value is less than 0.05 indicates that the data varies significantly from normality and/or equal variance, thus we would use the Spearman's rho. If the p-values are greater than 0.05 then we can assume that the assumptions have been met and our data meets the requirements of normality, allowing us to use Pearson's r.

Assumption checks
Shapiro-Wilk Test for Multivariate Normality

Shapiro-Wilk	p
0.807	< .001

Shapiro-Wilk Test for Bivariate Normality

		Shapiro-Wilk	p
Revise	- Exam	0.807	< .001

Quantitative Analysis

The assumptions for this data is not met, as shown by the assumption checks p-values are less than 0.05 (p < 0.001). The Spearman's rho correlation coefficient is appropriate to use in this case.

Review the p-Value. The second value in each row, labeled "p-value", will give the significance, or p-value, of the correlation Any correlation greater than +/-0.199 will be statistically significant.

Review the Correlation Coefficient. The first results table displays the correlation table were we will examine the Spearman's rho values.

Correlation Table

Variable		Revise	Exam
1. Revise	Pearson's r	—	
	p-value	—	
	Spearman's rho	—	
	p-value	—	
2. Exam	Pearson's r	0.397	—
	p-value	< .001	—
	Spearman's rho	0.350	—
	p-value	< .001	—

Spearman Correlation Table

The Spearman correlation value indicates the direction and strength of the association. In the example above we could state that the variables have a weak positive correlation, r = 0.350 (p < 0.01).

Report the Results. In Social Science research, results are typically reported using the American Psychological Association (APA) format.

Basic Format
r (N - 2) = Spearman's rho-value, p < 0.001
- N-2 is the sample size, found in the "n" row of the table minus 2.
- Spearman's rho-vale is located in the "Spearman's rho" row of the table.
- p represents the p-value in the "p" row.

Example report for this analysis.
There is a weak positive correlation (r_s = 0.350) between the age of an antique clock and the selling price of that clock at auction as shown by Spearman's rho coefficient.

Correlation Analysis with Rank Order Data (Nonparametric Example)

In the following examples we will be using the Fear of Statistics dataset from the JASP Library. This data comes from a fictious questionnaire that asked students about their views on math, statistics, and related topics. All items are on a 5-point Likert scale (1 = strongly disagree, 5 = strongly agree).

We will be asking the data if there is a correlation between a student's confidence in mathematics and computers use. In the survey, question seven (Q7) stated "All computers hate me". Question eight (Q8) stated "I have never been good at mathematics".

Open the Fear of Statistics dataset from the JASP data Library
Data Library > Categories > Reliability > Fear of Statistics

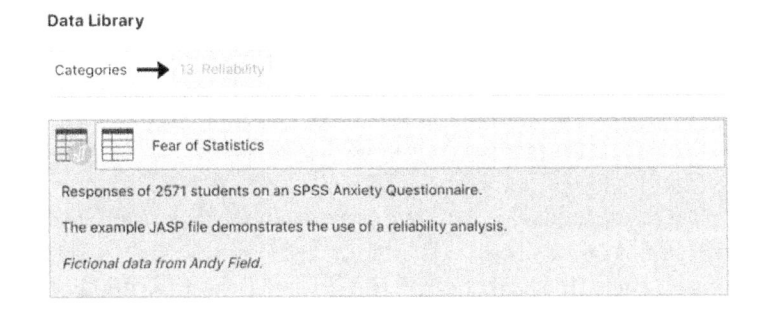

Use the Regression Tab, select Correlation Matrix. This will allow you to compare rank order data for an association . The Correlation Matrix test will perform a Spearman's Rank Order Correlation on the data. Spearman's correlation is used for Likert scale rank order data, as we have in this sample, as well as continuous non-parametric data.

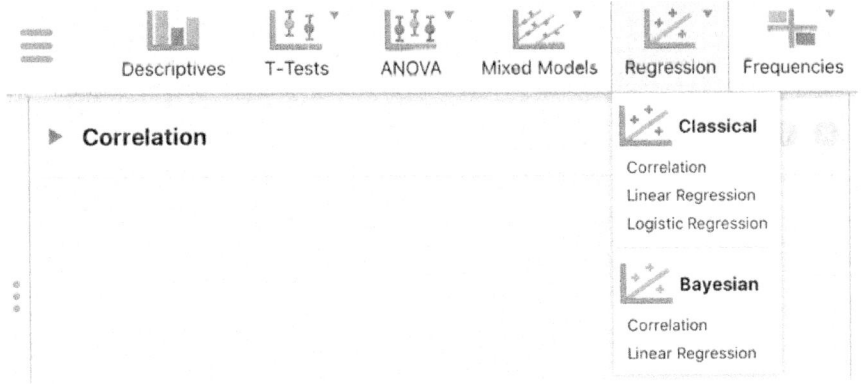

Bivariate Correlation Menu

From the dialog box move the two variables into the right-side column.

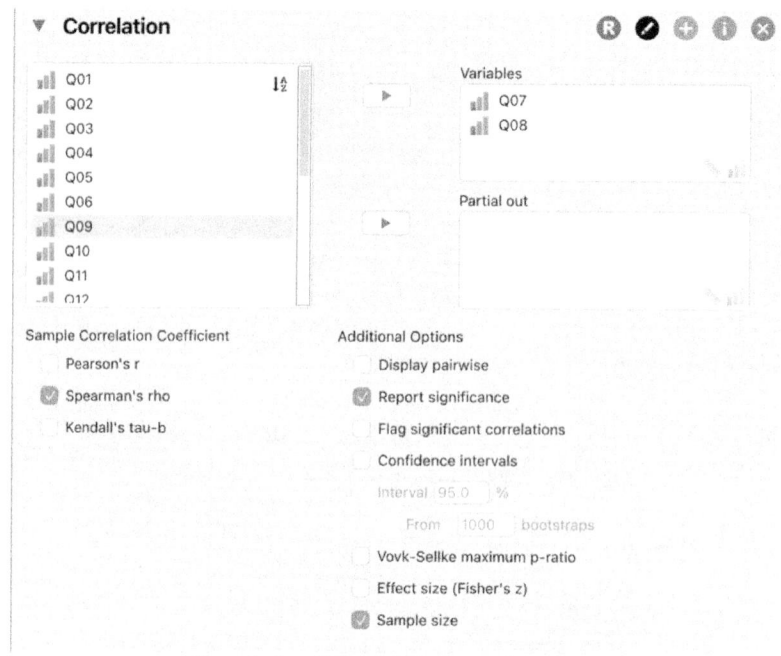

Correlation Matrix Dialogue Window

The other settings we will select are the Spearman Correlation Coefficient and Reporting the significance. The "Alt. Hypothesis" is simply "Correlated" since we do not have a hypothesis about the direction of the possible correlation. Our hypothesis is that a person's feelings towards mathematics and their feelings towards computers are simply correlated.

We should also use the Assumptions pull-down menu to check if these assumptions are met or not. However, since this is Likert-scale data, it will probably not meet any of the assumptions.

Interpreting Results Tables: Correlation Matrix (Fear of Statistics)

Check the Assumptions. When reviewing the results of the assumption checks tables, a p-value is less than 0.05 indicates that the data varies significantly from normality and/or equal variance, thus we would use the Spearman's rho. If the p-values are greater than 0.05 then we can assume that the assumptions have been met and our data meets the requirements of normality, allowing us to use Pearson's r.

Assumption checks
Shapiro-Wilk Test for Multivariate Normality

Shapiro-Wilk	p
0.957	< .001

Shapiro-Wilk Test for Bivariate Normality

		Shapiro-Wilk	p
Q07 - Q08		0.957	< .001

The assumptions for this data is not met, as shown by the assumption checks p-values are less than 0.05 (p < 0.001). The Spearman's rho correlation coefficient is appropriate to use in this case.

Review the p-Value. The second value in each row, labeled "p-value", will give the significance, or p-value, of the correlation Any correlation greater than +/-0.199 will be statistically significant.

Review the Correlation Coefficient. The first results table displays the Spearman's rho (r_s) correlation coefficient.

Spearman's Correlations

Variable		Q07	Q08
1. Q07	n	—	
	Spearman's rho	—	
	p-value	—	
2. Q08	n	2571	—
	Spearman's rho	0.292	—
	p-value	< .001	—

Spearman Correlation Table

The Spearman's correlation value indicates the direction and strength of the association. The second value in each row, labeled "p-value", will give the significance, or p-value, of the correlation. In the example above we could state that the variables have a weak positive correlation, $r_s = 0.292$ (p < 0.01).

The "r_s" symbol indicates that a Spearman's correlation test was used. The "s" subscript is the indicator for this analysis.

Report the Results. In Social Science research, results are typically reported using the American Psychological Association (APA) format.

Basic Format
r (N - 2) = Spearman's rho-value, p < 0.001
- N-2 is the sample size, found in the "n" row of the table minus 2.
- Spearman's rho-vale is located in the "Spearman's rho" row of the table.
- p represents the p-value in the "p" row.

Example report for this analysis.
There is a weak correlation (r_s = 0.292) between question 7 and question 8 of the survey as shown by Spearman's rho coefficient.

Chapter 9
Associations with Regression (Simple Linear)

When to use Simple Linear Regression – in plain English

We alluded to the purpose of a Simple Linear Regression in the previous chapter. If we know that our measurements approximate a line on a graph, then by using some straightforward and simple Algebra, well somewhat simple, then we can create an equation that can be used to take the known value of one variable and predict the value of the other variable. We can also use this equation to predict the amount our dependent variable will change based on how much the independent variable changes in the equation.

Regression

The purpose of regression analysis is to explore the associations between variables and to model those associations. The analysis will tell us how much one variable changes with respect to the other variable and provide us with an equation to predict the value of one variable from the other variable. The values can also be used to model the association between the variables.

Regression Analysis, typically Linear regression, is an approach for modeling the linear relationship between two variables. Linear regression is a basic and commonly used type of predictive analysis. The overall idea of regression is to examine if an independent variable(s) do a good job in predicting or modeling an outcome (dependent) variable and to determine which variables in particular are significant predictors of the outcome variable. These regression estimates are used to explain the relationship between one dependent variable and one or more independent variables. The simplest form of the regression equation contains one dependent and one independent variable.

Regression analysis is a reliable method of identifying which variables have impact on a topic of interest. The process of performing a regression allows you to confidently determine which factors matter most, which factors can be ignored, and how these factors influence each other.

The Standard Error represents the average distance that the observed values fall away from the regression line. We could say that it tells us how wrong or off the regression model is on average using the units of the variables being considered. Smaller values are better because it indicates that the observations are closer to the line of best fit.

Simple linear regression is a statistical method that allows us to summarize and study relationships between two continuous variables; one being thought of as the dependent variable and the other acting as the independent variable.

Basic Quantitative Analysis Process (Regression)

Check Appropriateness of Regression
- *Before performing a regression model, we must check that the data is appropriate for this method.*

Review the Model
- *Determine how much the independent variable accounts for changes in the dependent variable.*

Review for Statistical Significance
- *Ensure that the model is statistically significance.*

Review the Coefficients
- *The linear model will show how much the dependent variable changes with each unit of change in the independent variable.*

Report the Results
- *After the analysis, you will want to report the results. If the results were not significant, simply state that the results were "not statistically significant. Significant results are reported in a formal format.*

Simple Linear Regression Analysis

In the following examples we will be using the antique clock auction (Auction) data from the JASP Data Library. We will be asking the data if there is an association between the final price of the clock and the age of the clock?

Open the Exam Anxiety dataset from the JASP data Library
Data Library > Categories > Regression > Auction

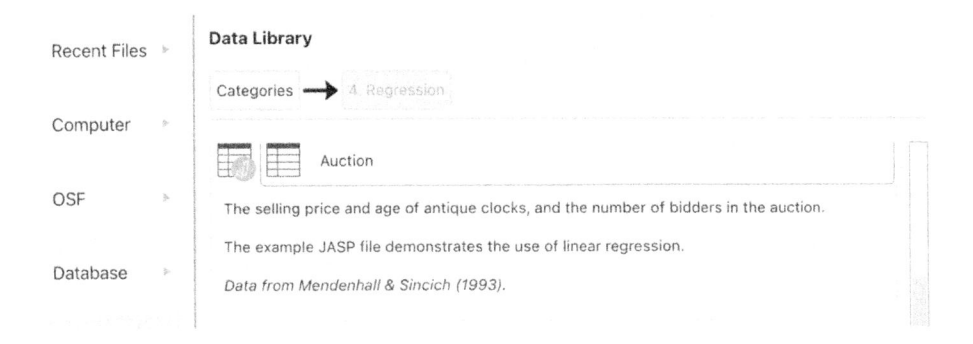

We must first ensure that a simple linear regression model is appropriate for the data. This can be accomplished with a correlation. When we have statistically significant correlations, then we can use that data in a simple linear regression.

In order to perform a regression analysis, from the JASP menu select Regression > Linear Regression.

Quantitative Analysis

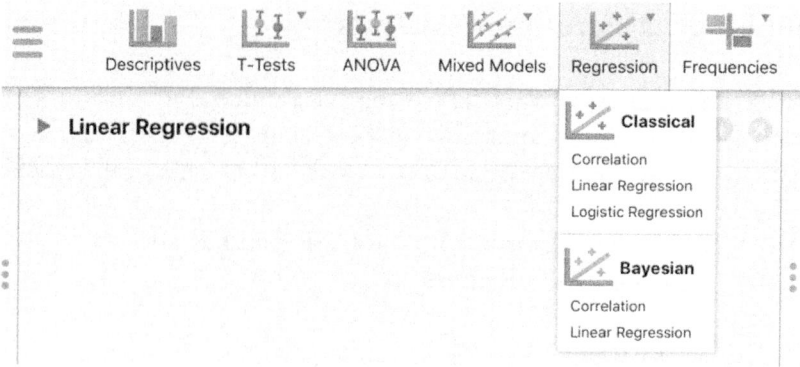

JASP Linear Regression Menu

Using the regression dialog box move one variable into the "Dependent" box and the other variable into the "Independent" box. In this example we have used the final selling price (Price) as the dependent variable and the age of the clock (Age) as the independent variable. By doing this our hypothesis is that we will be able to predict or model the final selling price based on the clock's age.

Select the dependent variable from the list of variables and use the selection arrow to move it into the dependent variable window. Then select the independent variable from the list and use the selection arrow to move it into the independent variable window.

Regression Dialogue Window

The other settings in the Regression dialogue window, such as Model, Statistics, Method Specification, and Plots, can remain on the default settings.

Interpreting Results Tables: Simple Linear Regression (Auction)

We will be able to examine the regression table in the output window of JASP. In this example we have a Regression output table to determine the linear equation to be used to predict an antique clock's final selling price from the clock's age. We can also make claims about how much we can expect the selling price to increase for each "unit" increase (each additional year older) in the clock's age.

Linear Regression Results Tables

Model Summary - Price

Model	R	R²	Adjusted R²	RMSE
H₀	0.000	0.000	0.000	393.134
H₁	0.730	0.533	0.518	273.028

ANOVA

Model		Sum of Squares	df	Mean Square	F	p
H₁	Regression	$2.555 \times 10^{+6}$	1	$2.555 \times 10^{+6}$	34.273	<.001
	Residual	$2.236 \times 10^{+6}$	30	74544.507		
	Total	$4.791 \times 10^{+6}$	31			

Note. The intercept model is omitted, as no meaningful information can be shown.

Coefficients

Model		Unstandardized	Standard Error	Standardized	t	p
H₀	(Intercept)	1327.156	69.497		19.097	<.001
H₁	(Intercept)	-191.658	263.887		-0.726	0.473
	Age	10.479	1.790	0.730	5.854	<.001

Regression Output Table

Check Appropriateness of Regression. A simple linear regression model should only be used with data that has a statistically significant correlation. The stronger the correlation, the more reliable the regression model.

Pearson's Correlations

Variable		Price	Age
1. Price	Pearson's r	—	
	p-value	—	
2. Age	Pearson's r	0.730	—
	p-value	<.001	—

The selling price and the clock's age have a strong positive correlation (r = 0.730) and is statistically significant. It is appropriate to use this data in a simple linear regression model.

Quantitative Analysis

Review the Model. The model summary table will show the Pearson R-value that we obtained from our Correlation, seen in the Model Summary column "R". The Pearson r tells us that there is a strong positive correlation between the clock's age and final selling price.

The "R-Squared" (R^2) value indicates how much of the variance is accounted for by the association. In this case we find an R^2 value of 0.533, telling us that approximately 53.3% of the variance in the data is due to the association between the selling price of the clock and the age of the clock. The higher the R-squared value the stronger the association between the data sets.

Model Summary - Price

Model	R	R^2	Adjusted R^2	RMSE
H_0	0.000	0.000	0.000	393.134
H_1	0.730	0.533	0.518	273.028

Model Summary for Math and Reading

Review the Statistical Significance. The regression output table will also produce an ANOVA table for the data. In this case we find an F-value of 34.2 (df 1,30) is statistically significant ($p < 0.001$).

ANOVA

Model		Sum of Squares	df	Mean Square	F	p
H_1	Regression	$2.555 \times 10^{+6}$	1	$2.555 \times 10^{+6}$	34.273	< .001
	Residual	$2.236 \times 10^{+6}$	30	74544.507		
	Total	$4.791 \times 10^{+6}$	31			

ANOVA Table from Regression

Review the Coefficients. The Coefficients table gives us the coefficients to model the association between the dependent variable and the independent variable. The values for the linear equation are obtained from the "B" column of the coefficients output table, shown here in the "Unstandardized" column.

Coefficients

Model		Unstandardized	Standard Error	Standardized	t	p
H_0	(Intercept)	1327.156	69.497		19.097	< .001
H_1	(Intercept)	-191.658	263.887		-0.726	0.473
	Age	10.479	1.790	0.730	5.854	< .001

Coefficients Table

The "Coefficients" table provides the values to use in a linear equation that will model the association between the variables. In this example the model was to show the relationship between the clock's age as the independent variable and final selling price as the dependent variable.

In this example, for every year increase in the clock's age, we would expect a $10.48 increase in the final selling price. Since we are using the unstandardized beta (B), the change in price based on the change in age can be expressed in the units used in the data. The units used are "age in years" for the clock's age (Age) and "dollars" for the final selling price (Price).

The linear equation that models this associations would be written as follows;

$$Price = -191.66 + (10.48 * Age)$$

The standard error for the unstandardized beta (*SE B*) is similar to the standard deviation for a mean. The larger the number, the more spread out the points are from the regression line. The more spread out the numbers are, the less likely that significance will be found. In our model the standard error is 1.79, which can be thought of as an expected or average error of $1.79 on the price when comparing the predicted selling price versus the actual selling price. The standard error gives a concrete sense of the precision we should expect from the linear regression model.

Report the Results. In Social Science research, results are typically reported using the American Psychological Association (APA) format.

Basic Format
So, I have bad news for you. The APA does not have any direct guidance on how to report regression analysis in a narrative format. Below is one suggestion for a narrative reporting for regression.

Example report for this analysis.
The results of the linear regression indicated that an antique clock's age explained 53.3% of the variance in the final selling price of an antique clock (R^2=.533). It was found that the age of a clock (p < 0.001) predicted the selling price. The unstandardized coefficient (*B*) indicates that for a 1-year increase in the antique clock's age, we observed a $10.48 increase in clock's final selling price at auction.

Chapter 10
Relationship Analysis with Contingency Tables

When to Use Contingency Tables – in plain English

In the simplest terms, contingency tables are used when you do not have numbers. This sounds odd since earlier we said that in JASP, all the data is changed into numbers for analysis. In this case, if we are comparing two variables that name some grouping and then those names were converted into numbers. We are talking about categorical data here. If this is the sort of data that is being analyzed, then contingency tables and the Chi Square analysis are the way to go.

What is a Contingency Table?

Contingency tables, also called crosstabs, are often used in statistics to summarize the relationship between categorical variables. A contingency table is a special type of frequency distribution table, where two variables are shown at the same time. The most common variables used in a contingency table are categorical, nominal factors. It is used when you have changed the names of things into numerical values for analysis.

The Contingency Table can display the Categorical variables as counts, or the percentages can also be displayed. The table can aid in detecting differences or relationships in a visual format. Chi Square analysis is the main feature of a contingency table. There are two main functions of the Chi Square analysis; goodness of fit and test of independence.

Goodness of fit will enable the researcher to compare the observed, or collected, data with the expected outcomes. Here we are interested in any differences between the observed and expected outcomes. This chapter does not go into the Goodness of Fit test.

Test of independence is focused in whether or not the values or factors are independent of one another. This is a type of correlation between the nominal factors. We are interested if the factors are "independent' from one another or if as one factor changes does the other factor change as well.

We also have the **contingency coefficient** available in JASP. The contingency coefficient is a coefficient of association that tells whether two variables or data sets are independent or dependent with respect to each other.

Chi-Square Analysis – Test of Independence

The Chi Square analysis test of independence method is used to find differences between categorical data items within the Contingency Table. The JASP Results window will produce a Contingency table that can be compared across the rows and down the columns for differences in the data. The following examples will use the Healthy Habits dataset from the JASP Data Library. This data comes from Seo, D.-C., Nehl, E., Agley, J., and Ma, S.-M. (2007). Relations between physical activity and behavioral and perceptual correlates among midwestern college students. *Journal of American College Health*, 56: 187-197. Health Habits data provides physical activity and consumption of fruits of 1184 college students.

The question we are asking of this data is whether or not there is a relationship between a student's physical activity level and the amount of fruit they consume.

Basic Quantitative Analysis Process (Chi Square)

Review for Statistical Significance
- *A p-value less than 0.05 is accepted as statistically significant in the Social Sciences.*
- *A p-value grater or equal to 0.05 is accepted as not statistically significant in the Social Sciences.*
- *If the result is statistically significant, go to the next steps. If a result is not statistically significant, the next steps are not necessary.*

Review the Effect Size
- *The effect size will provide information about the magnitude or how obvious the reported differences are in the real world and in the context of the data.*

Review the Contingency Table
- *The table will display expected results, if the data was independent, as well as the actual results.*
- *Review the table cells to determine if any actual values deviate from the expected.*

Report the Results
- *After the analysis, you will want to report the results. If the results were not significant, simply state that the results were "not statistically significant. Significant results are reported in a formal format.*

Using the Contingency Tables in JASP

Open the Health Habits dataset from the JASP data Library
Data Library > Categories > Frequencies > Health Habits

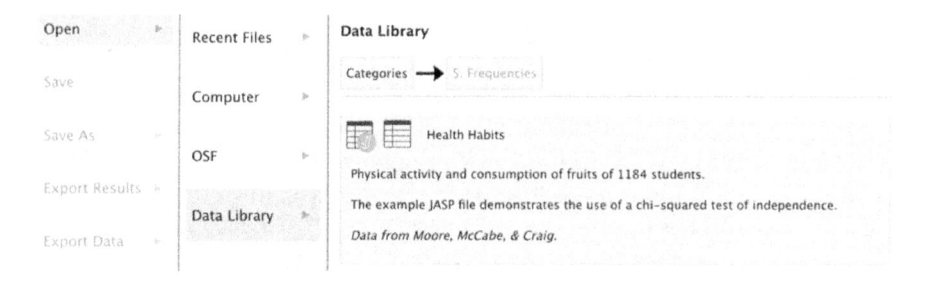

Using the Frequencies tab, select "Contingency Table".

JASP Contingency Table Function

In the dialog box select one of the categorical variables for the row and another categorical variable for the column. In this example we are interested in creating a Contingency table to examine the differences in Physical Activity (Low, Moderate, Vigorous) and fruit consumption by the participants (Low, Moderate, High).

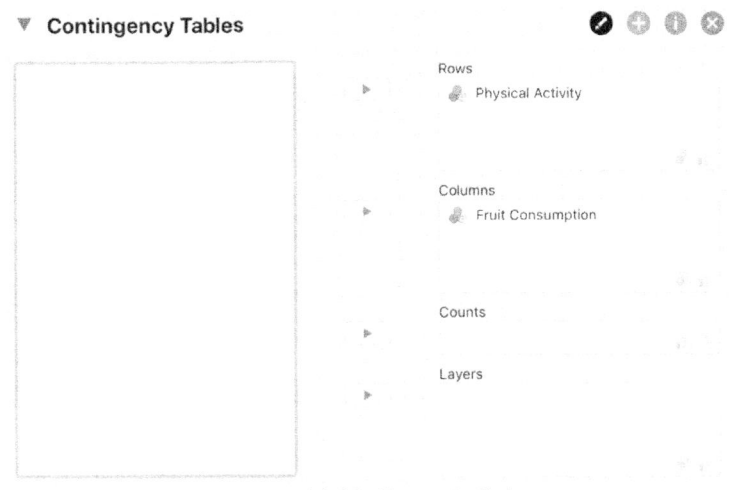

Contingency Table Rows & Columns

We are interested in whether or not there is a relationship between physical activity and fruit consumption. Since the differences we are interested in examining are based on "Physical Activity", this factor can be placed in the Rows section. "Fruit Consumption" is the factor that we expect to see these differences, so it can be placed in the columns section. When using Contingency Tables, the order of variables in rows and columns does not really matter.

Using the "Statistics" setting in the dialogue window, select the Chi Square test ($\chi 2$) as well as "Phi and Cramer's V" to measure effect size. The Chi Square test will provide us with the p-values for differences in the data while the Phi and Cramer's V will show the effect size of those differences.

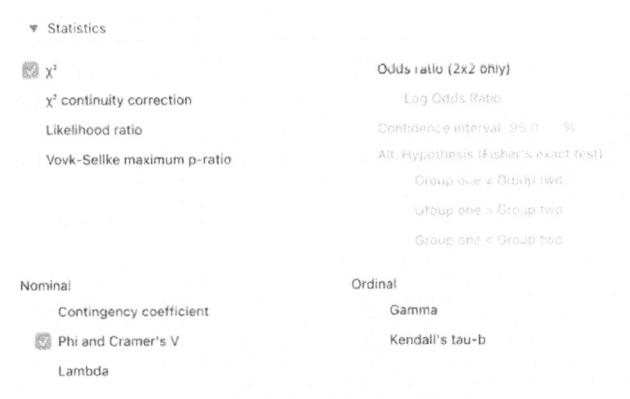

Statistics Selection Window

When the factors used for the Chi Square analysis produce a 2X2 Contingency Table, that is both factors contained two groups, it is recommended that we use the "χ^2 continuity correction" setting. It has been shown that Chi Square methods can produce an overestimation of relationships in 2X2 tables. The continuity correction accounts for this overestimation.

In the Cells section of the window, it is helpful for the results table to display Observed counts as well as the Expected counts. This will give us the overall counts contained in the data and the counts that the Chi Square analysis expected if there were no differences within the data groupings.

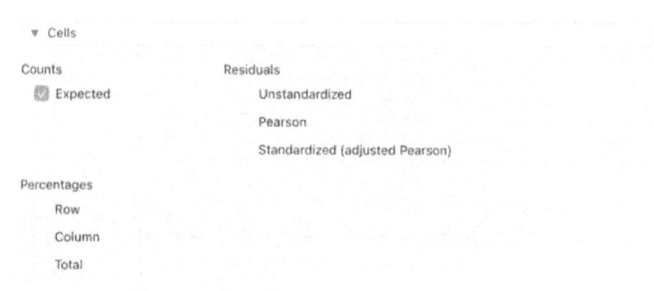

Observed and Expected Counts Setting

A Chi Square analysis "expects" a count of at least 5 in each cell. If any of the cells contain an expected count smaller than 5, then the Chi Square analysis assumption has been violated and the test may not have been appropriate for this data.

The JASP Results window will produce three tables: the Contingency Table, the Chi Square test results, and the Nominal Table containing Phi and Cramer's V measures of effect size.

Interpreting Results Tables: Contingency Table Analysis (Health Habits)

The Contingency Table does a very good job of indicating if there are statistically significant relationships or differences within the categorical data. The Chi-square test itself can only indicate there are some differences. We also need to examine the Contingency Table to uncover where those differences may be present.

Let's take a look at the Contingency Table results when asking whether there is a relationship between a student's physical activity and fruit consumption.

Review for Statistical Significance. In our example we conducted a chi-square analysis to determine if there are any relationships between a student's physical activity (low, moderate, or vigorous) and their fruit consumption (low, medium, or high). The JASP results window shows that there is a statistically significant relationship between a student's physical activity level and their fruit consumption habits, x^2 (4, N=1184) = 14.15, p = 0.007.

Chi-Squared Tests

	Value	df	p
X²	14.15	4	0.007
N	1184		

Chi-square tests

Review the Effect Size. The Nominal table also provides us with some insights about the effect size of these differences.

Nominal

	Value[a]
Phi-coefficient	NaN
Cramer's V	0.077

[a] Value could not be calculated - At least one row or column contains all zeros

Effect Size Coefficients Table

The Cramer's V value indicates that there is a small effect size.

Effect Size Calculation	Statistics Test	Small Effect	Medium Effect	Large Effect
Phi or Cramer's Phi	Chi Squared	0.1	0.3	0.5

Values from Cohen (1988) Statistical Power Analysis for the Behavioral Sciences

Review the Contingency Table. But this is only part of the story. In the above example there are three categories for the physical activity level and three categories for fruit consumption. How do we determine the significant differences?

One way to go about answering this question is by analyzing the Contingency Table that is also produced in the JASP Results window.

Contingency Tables

Physical Activity		Fruit Consumption			Total
		Low	Medium	High	
Low	Count	69.00	25.00	14.00	108.00
	Expected count	51.90	29.28	26.81	108.00
Moderate	Count	206.00	126.00	111.00	443.00
	Expected count	212.89	120.10	110.00	443.00
Vigorous	Count	294.00	170.00	169.00	633.00
	Expected count	304.20	171.61	157.18	633.00
Total	Count	569.00	321.00	294.00	1184.00
	Expected count	569.00	321.00	294.00	1184.00

Contingency Table showing Observed and Expected counts

Quantitative Analysis

Notice that in the Contingency table each row contains two lines. The first line indicates the count for that particular cell and the second line tells us the expected count if there were no differences.

Contingency Tables

Physical Activity		Fruit Consumption			
		Low	Medium	High	Total
Low	Count	69.00	25.00	14.00	108.00
	Expected count	51.90	29.28	26.81	108.00

Contingency Table Observed Count

When we read Line 1 of the row, we know that from the population in the low physical activity group that 69 had low fruit consumption, 25 had medium fruit consumption, and 14 had high fruit consumption. We also know that there was a total of 108 low physical activity students in this analysis.

The observed counts and expected counts can be compared. In the case of the low physical activity group, we find that there is a noticeable difference between the counts in the Low and High fruit consumption groups.

Contingency Tables

Physical Activity		Fruit Consumption			
		Low	Medium	High	Total
Low	Count	69.00	25.00	14.00	108.00
	Expected count	51.90	29.28	26.81	108.00

Contingency Table Count Comparison

In this example we can state that participants with low physical activity levels tended to consumer less fruit than expected. We can make this broad statement from the low physical activity group since their low fruit consumption was more than we expected and their high fruit consumption was less than we expected.

The other student physical activity groups can be examined in much the same manner.

Contingency Tables

Physical Activity		Fruit Consumption			
		Low	Medium	High	Total
Moderate	Count	206.00	126.00	111.00	443.00
	Expected count	212.89	120.10	110.00	443.00

Contingency Table of Moderate Physical Activity group

The moderate physical activity student group has observed counts that are close to the expected counts. The values do not seem very different from one another.

Contingency Tables

Physical Activity		Fruit Consumption			
		Low	Medium	High	Total
Vigorous	Count	294.00	170.00	169.00	633.00
	Expected count	304.20	171.61	157.18	633.00

Contingency Table of Vigorous Physical Activity group

The vigorous physical activity student group shows unexpected higher counts in the High fruit consumption category. This would suggest that students who engage in vigorous physical activity tend to consume more fruit than expected.

When the entire contingency table is considered, the overarching result could be summed up by stating that participants with low physical activity levels tended to consume less fruit and participants engaged in vigorous physical activity tended to consume more fruit.

Report the Results. In Social Science research, results are typically reported using the American Psychological Association (APA) format.

Basic Format
χ^2 (df, N = sample size) = Chi^2 value, p = "actual p-value unless <0.001", with a _____ effect size (ϕ = Phi or Cramer's Phi value).

Example report for this analysis.
The difference in fruit consumption based on physical activity was statistically significant, χ^2 (4, 1184) = 14.15, p = .007, with a small effect (ϕ = 0.077). People with low physical activity has a lower than expected amount of fruit consumption while those with vigorous physical activity had a higher than expected amount of fruit consumption.

Quantitative Analysis

Section IV: Resources

Analysis Memos

The purpose of writing an analysis memo is to keep all your analyses organized and to have written documentation of all the analysis you do. This way you will know what paths you went down, which ones lead to interesting places, and you will have the writing to include in your dissertation/paper when needed.

I. Question
This is expressed in terms that can be answered with our data. (ie. Are there gender differences in responses to questions X,Y,Z?)

II. Method. (ie. summation of frequency counts, correlation, ...)
Include a rationalization for using this type of analysis if necessary.

III. Results.
Include tables and/or charts with results that could be input into formal writing if needed.

IV. Discussion.
Thoughts or reactions to results. Can be formal or informal writing.

Sample Analysis Memo

I. Question: Are there SES differences in school types?

II. Method: A chi-square test of group difference was conducted on SES, with three categories, by School type, with two categories.

III. Results: The chi-square test of group differences was significant ($X^2 (2) = 6.33$, $p = .04$), indicating that there are statistically significant group differences in SES by type of school.

Type of School by SES

School Type	SES Low	Middle	High
	N (% w/School Type)		
Public	45 (26.8%)	76 (45.2%)	47 (28%)
Private	2 (6.3%)	19 (59.4%)	11 (34.4%)

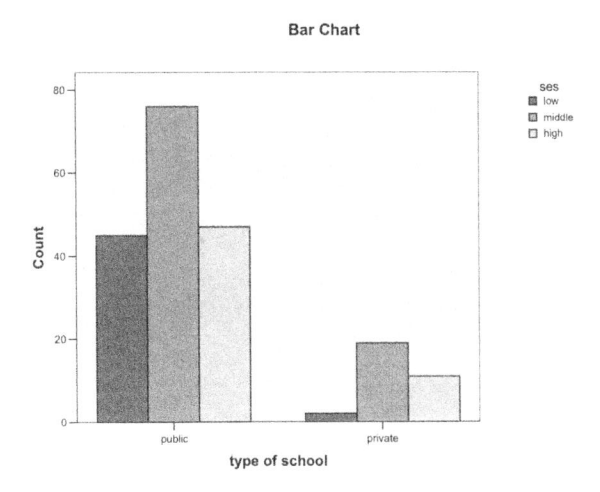

Bar Chart

IV. Discussion: Although the majority of students from all three SES groups attend public school, fewer low income students attend private school than any other SES groups, while more middle income students attend private school than any other SES groups. This is an interesting finding as one might assume that students from high SES backgrounds would be more likely to attend private schools. I wonder if this could be due to higher SES families living in school districts with better public schools, while middle income families may not have access to the best public schools, but do have the financial means to send their children to private schools.

Data Sets used in the Guide

Directed Reading Activities

Description: This data set, "Directed Reading Activities", provides reading performance of two groups of pupils - one control group and one group that was given Directed Reading Activities (Moore et al, 2012, p. 432).

Variables:
- id - Identification number of a pupil.
- group - Experimental group indicator ('Treatment' = participation in the Directed Reading Activities, 'Control' = Control group).
- g - Experimental group indicator expressed as a binary variable (0= Directed Reading Activities, 1= Control group).
- drp - The performance on Degree of Reading Power test.

In this example JASP file, we will compare two classrooms of students with the aim of testing the null hypothesis that Directed Reading Activities (only in one of the classes) do not enhance the performance of pupils on Degree of Reading Power test (DRP).

References:
D. S. Moore, G. P. McCabe, and B. A. Craig. (2012). *Introduction to the Practice of Statistics* (7th ed.). New York: Freeman.

Schmitt, M. C. (1978). The effects of an elaborated directed reading activity on the meta-comprehension skills of third graders. *PhD thesis*, Purdue University.

Horizontal Eye Movements

Description: This data set, "Horizontal Eye Movements", provides the number of recalled words by two groups of participants - during the retention interval, one group was instructed to fixate on a centrally presented dot; the other group was instructed to execute horizontal saccades.

Specifically, "Participants were presented with a list of neutral study words for a subsequent free recall test. Prior to recall, participants were requested to perform - depending on the experimental condition - either horizontal, vertical, or no eye movements (i.e., looking at a central fixation point). The type of eye movement was thus manipulated between subjects. As the effect of eye movement on episodic memory has been reported to be influenced by handedness, we tested only strong right-handed individuals. The dependent variable of interest was the number of correctly recalled words." (Matzke et al, 2015, p. 3)

This data set contains only data from participants assigned to the horizontal and no eye movements condition.

Variables:
- ParticipantNumber - Participant's identification number.
- Condition - Experimental condition (Fixed = fixed gaze, Horizontal = horizontal eye movements).
- CriticalRecall - The number of Recalled words after the memory retrieval task.

Reference:
Matzke, D., Nieuwenhuis, S., van Rijn, H., Slagter, H. A., van der Molen, M. W., and Wagenmakers, E.-J. (2015). The effect of horizontal eye movements on free recall: A preregistered adversarial collaboration. *Journal of Experimental Psychology: General*: 144:e1-e15.

Moon and Aggression

Description: This data set, "Moon & Aggression", provides the number of disruptive behaviors by dementia patients during two different phases of the lunar cycle (Moore et al, 2012, p. 410). Each row corresponds to one participant.

Variables:
- Moon - The average number of disruptive behaviors during full moon days.
- Other - The average number of disruptive behaviors during other days.

This example JASP file demonstrates the use of paired samples *t*-test. Specifically, we will examine the adequacy of the null hypothesis which states that the average number of disruptive behaviors among patients with dementia does not differ between moon days and other days.

References:
Moore, D. S., McCabe, G. P., and Craig. B. A. (2012) *Introduction to the Practice of Statistics* (7th ed). New York: Freeman.

"These data were collected as part of a larger study of dementia patients conducted by Nancy Edwards and Alan Beck, Purdue University." (Moore et al, 2012, p. N-8).

Pain Thresholds

Description: This data set, "Pain thresholds", provides pain threshold for people with different hair color.

Variables:
- V1 - Participant number.
- Hair Color - Hair color of the participant (`Light Blond' = light blond, `Dark Blond' = dark blond, `Light Brunette' = light brunette, `Dark Brunette' = dark brunette).
- Pain Tolerance - Performance on pain sensitivity test (the higher the score, the better the pain tolerance).

This example JASP file demonstrates the use of one-way ANOVA.

Reference:
McClave, J. T. and Dietrich, F. H. (1991). *Statistics*. San Francisco: Dellen publishing.

Auction

Description: This data set, "Auction", provides the selling price and age of antique clocks, and the number of bidders in the auction.

Variables:
- Age - Age of the antique clock.
- Bidders - The number of bidders in the auction.
- Price - The final selling price of the clock.

This example JASP file demonstrates the use of Bayesian linear regression. Specifically, we are interested whether and to what extent the age of the clocks and the number of bidders in the auction predict the final selling price.

Reference:
Mendenhall, W, and Sincich, TL (1993). *A Second Course in Statistics: Regression Analysis* (6th ed.), New Jersey: Prentice-Hall.

Facebook Friends

Description:

This data set, "Facebook Friends", provides preference ratings for Facebook profiles - five groups judge the same facebook profiles, except for the one aspect that was manipulated: the number of friends for that profile.

Variables:

- **Friends** - Experimental group - number of friends (the number indicates the number of friended accounts with the mockup profile).
- **Participant** - Participant number.
- **Score** - Social attractiveness rating of the mockup profile (1 = lowest rating, 7 = highest rating).

References:

D. S. Moore, G. P. McCabe, and B A. Craig. *Introduction to the practice of statistics* (7th. ed). New York: Freeman.

Stephanie Tom Tong, Brandon Van Der Heide, Lindsey Langwell, Joseph B. Walther; Too Much of a Good Thing? The Relationship between Number of Friends and Interpersonal Impressions on Facebook, *Journal of Computer-Mediated Communication*, 13(3), 2008.

Health Habits

Description: This data set, "Health Habits", provides physical activity and consumption of fruits of 1184 students.
Variables:

- Physical Activity - Physical activity of the participant (Low, Moderate, Vigorous).
- Fruit Consumption - Participant's consumption of fruits (Low, Medium, High).

This example JASP file demonstrates the use of a Chi-squared test of independence. Specifically, we assess the adequacy of the null hypothesis that physical activity and fruit consumption are independent.

Reference:

Moore, D. S., McCabe, G. P., and Craig, B. A. (2012). *Introduction to the Practice of Statistics* (7th ed.). New York: Freeman.

Seo, D.-C., Nehl, E., Agley, J., and Ma, S.-M. (2007). Relations between physical activity and behavioral and perceptual correlates among midwestern college students. *Journal of American College Health*, 56: 187-197.

Effect Size Tables

Effect Size Magnitude Table

Effect Size Calculation	Statistics Test	Small Effect	Medium Effect	Large Effect
Phi or Cramer's Phi	Chi Squared	0.1	0.3	0.5
Cohen's d	t-Test (Paired & Independent)	0.2	0.5	0.8
Eta Squared	ANOVA	0.01	0.06	0.14
r	Correlation	0.1	0.3	0.5
r²	Correlation and t-Test (Independent)	0.01	0.09	0.25

Values from Cohen (1988) Statistical Power Analysis for the behavioral Sciences

Effect Size Calculation Equations

Effect Size Calculation	Statistics Test	Equation	Notes
Phi (φ)	Chi Squared 2X2	$\varphi = \sqrt{\frac{\chi^2}{N}}$	N is the total number of observations.
Cramer's Phi (φ_c)	Chi Squared > 2X2	$\varphi_c = \sqrt{\frac{\chi^2}{N(k-1)}}$	N is the total number of observations and k is the lesser of rows or columns.
Cohen's d	t-Test (Paired)	$d = \frac{mean_2 - mean_1}{standard\ deviation\ (SD)}$	
Cohen's d	t-Test (Independent)	$d = \frac{mean_2 - mean_1}{SD_{pooled}}$	SD pooled = $\sqrt{\frac{(SD_{group1})^2 + (SD_{group2})^2}{2}}$
Eta Squared	ANOVA	$\eta^2 = \frac{SS_{between\ groups}}{SS_{total}}$	
r	Correlation and t-Test (Independent)	$r = \sqrt{\frac{t^2}{(t^2 + df)}}$	Correlation output tables will show the r-value.
r²	Correlation and t-Test (Independent)	$r^2 = \frac{t^2}{(t^2 + df)}$	Correlation output tables will show the r²-value.

Reporting Frequentist Statistics

Statistic	Data	Questions	Reporting
t-Test; Independent Samples Example *One-Sample and Paired Sample reporting follows similar format.*	Continuous Dependent Variable (Real or Interval number) with a Categorical Factor with only 2 groups (Nominal or Ordinal)	Are student **writing scores** different based on their **gender**?	Student's t-Test: The differences in writing scores based on gender were statistically significant, t(198) = -14.89, p < 0.001 (d = -2.23), as shown by the Student's t-test. Female students scored approximately 5 points higher than boys in this study, with a 95% confidence interval for the mean difference being from 2 to 7 points difference, 95% CI [2, 7]. *t*(df) = t-value, *p* < .001 (d = Cohen's d value). Report details about the 95% CI. Welch t-Test: The differences in writing assessment scores between girls and boys is statistically significant, t(169.7) = -3.66, p < 0.001 with a medium effect size (d = -0.525), as shown by Welch's test. Female students scored approximately 5 points higher than boys in this study, with a 95% confidence interval for the mean difference being from 2 to 7 points difference, 95% CI [2, 7]. *t*(df) = t-value, *p* < .001 (d = Cohen's d value). Report details about the 95% CI.
ANOVA	Continuous Dependent Variable (Real or Interval number) with a Categorical	Are student **writing scores** different based on their	Standard One-Way ANOVA: The differences in writing assessment scores between different academic programs is statistically significant, F(2, 197) = 21.275, p < 0.001 with

	Factors with 3 or more groups (Nominal or Ordinal)	**program type enrollment?**	a large effect size ($\eta^2 = 0.178$), as shown by the One-Way ANOVA. The academic program outperformed the general program by approximately 5 points 95% CI [-8.7, -1.2] and the vocational program by approximately 9 points 95% CI [5.9, 13.0]. The general program outperformed the vocational program by approximately 4 points 95% CI [0.3, 8.7]. F(df, residual df) = F-value, p = ____, with a ____ effect size (partial eta squared/eta squared). Report details about the 95% CI. Kruskal-Wallis: The differences in reading assessment scores between different race groups is statistically significant, H(3) = 17.07, p < 0.001, as shown by the Kruskal-Wallis test. The students identified as white outperformed the students identified as Hispanic by approximately 8 points 95% CI [13.3, -2.8] and the students identified as African-American by approximately 11 points, 95% CI [-11.8, -0.3]. H(df) = H-value, p = ____ with an ___ effect size (partial eta squared/eta squared). Report details about the 95% CI.
Correlation	Continuous Data, Interval or Discreet	Is there a correlation between the student's **reading scores** and	The students reading and math scores showed a strong positive correlation, r(198) = 0.66, p < 0.001.

Quantitative Analysis

		math scores?	$r(N-2)$ = Pearson's r-value, $p < 0.001$
Simple Linear Regression	Continuous Data, Interval or Discreet	Can a student's **social studies scores** be predicted from their **reading scores**?	The results of the linear regression indicated the reading grades explained 47% of the variance in Social Studies grades ($R^2=.471$). It was found that reading grades ($p < 0.001$) predicted social studies grades. The unstandardized coefficient (B) indicates that for a 1 point increase in reading score, we observed a .4 increase in social studies scores. B = unstandardized Beta for math, p-value, and R^2.
Chi Square, Crosstabs, Contingency Tables	Only Categorical Data, i.e. Nominal and Ordinal	Are there differences in **school type enrollment** based on a student's **SES group**?	The difference in percentage of program enrollment based on SES was statistically significant, $\chi^2 (1, N = 200) = 15.5, p = .02$, with a medium effect ($\phi = .50$). χ^2 (df, N = sample size) = Chi² value, p = "'actual p-value unless <0.001", with a medium effect (ϕ = Phi or Cramer's Phi value)

Interpreting Effect Size

t-Test uses Cohen's d for effect size
- Small effect = 0.2
- Medium Effect = 0.5
- Large Effect = 0.8

ANOVA uses eta squared (η^2) or partial eta squared (η^2_p) for effect size
- Small = 0.01
- Medium = 0.06
- Large = 0.14

Correlation uses the r-coefficient or Spearman's rho for effect size
- -/+ .09 to 0 is no correlation
- -/+ .1 to .29 is a very weak correlation
- -/+ .3 to .49 is a weak correlation
- -/+ .5 to .69 is a moderate correlation
- -/+ .7 to 1.0 is a strong correlation

References

Beavers, A. S., Lounsbury, J. W., Richards, J. K., Huck, S. W., Skolits, G J., & Esquivel, S. L. (2013). Practical considerations for using exploratory factor analysis in educational research. Practical Assessment, Research & Evaluation, 18(6), 1-13. Retrieved from http://www.pareonline.net/pdf/v18n6.pdf

Cohen, J. (1988). Statistical power analysis for the behavioral sciences (2nd ed). Hillsdale, N.J: L. Erlbaum Associates.

Conway, J. M., & Huffcutt, A. I. (2003). A review and evaluation of exploratory factor analysis practices in organizational research. Organizational Research Methods, 6, 147-168. doi:10.1177/1094428103251541

DeCoster, J. (1998). Overview of Factor Analysis. Retrieved from http://www.stat-help.com/factor.pdf

Eagle, E., & Carroll, C. D. (1988). High school and beyond national longitudinal study: postsecondary enrollment, persistence, and attainment for 1972, 1980, and 1982 high school graduates. Washington, D.C: National Center for Education Statistics, U.S. Dept. of Education, Office of Educational Research and Improvement

Fabrigar, L. R., Wegener, D. T., MacCallum, R. C. & Strahan, E J. (1999). Evaluating the use of exploratory factor analysis in psychological research. Psychological Methods, 4, 272-299. doi:1082-989X/99/S3.00

Fisher, R. A. The Design of Experiments. Oliver and Boyd, Edinburgh, 1935.

Kline, R. B. (2004). Beyond significance testing: reforming data analysis methods in behavioral research (1st ed). Washington, DC: American Psychological Association.

Hayton, J. C., Allen, D. G., & Scarpello, V. (2004). Factor Retention Decisions in Exploratory Factor Analysis: a Tutorial on Parallel Analysis. Organizational Research Methods, 7(2), 191–205. https://doi.org/10.1177/1094428104263675

Howell, D. C. (1982). Statistical methods for psychology. Boston, Mass: Duxbury Press.

Jeffreys, H. (1961). Theory of probability (3rd Ed.). Oxford, UK: Oxford University Press.

Lee, M.D., & Wagenmakers, E.-J. (2013). Bayesian Modeling for Cognitive Science: A Practical Course: Cambridge University Press

National Governors Association Center for Best Practices, Council of Chief State School Officers (2010). Common Core State. National Governors Association Center for Best Practices, Council of Chief State School Officers, Washington D.C.

Raffery, A. E. (1995). Bayesian model selection in social research. In P. V. Marsden (Ed.), Sociological methodology 1995 (pp. 111–196). Cambridge, MA: Blackwell.

Schmitt, T. A. (2011). Current methodological considerations in exploratory and confirmatory factor analysis. Journal of Psychoeducational Assessment, 29(4), 304-321. doi:10.1177/0734282911406653

Wasserman, L. (2004). All of statistics: A concise course in statistical inference. New York: Springer.

Wetzels, R., Matzke, D., Lee, M. D., Rouder, J. N., Iverson, G. J., & Wagenmakers, E.-J. (2011). Statistical Evidence in Experimental Psychology: An Empirical Comparison Using 855 t Tests. Perspectives on Psychological Science, 6(3), 291–298. https://doi.org/10.1177/1745691611406923

ABOUT THE AUTHOR

Christopher P. Halter, Ed.D, is a faculty member at the University of California San Diego's Department of Education Studies. He teaches courses in mathematics education, secondary mathematics methods, research methodology, emerging technologies, and statistical analysis. His research includes teacher development, new teacher assessment, digital storytelling, and video analysis. He also teaches online courses in creating online collaborative communities, middle school science strategies, and blended & synchronous learning design. Dr. Halter has designed and taught Quantitative Analysis courses at both the graduate and undergraduate levels.

Printed in Great Britain
by Amazon